P9-DHF-698

CITY KID

ALSO BY NELSON GEORGE

NONFICTION

Post-Soul Nation

Hip Hop America

Buppies, B-boys, Baps, & Bohos

Blackface

Elevating the Game

The Death of Rhythm & Blues

Where Did Our Love Go?

WITH RUSSELL SIMMONS

Life and Def

FICTION

The Accidental Hunter

Night Work

Show & Tell

One Woman Short

Seduced

Urban Romance

NELSON GEORGE

CITY KID

A WRITER'S MEMOIR OF GHETTO LIFE AND POST-SOUL SUCCESS

VIKING

VIKING
Published by the Penguin Group
Penguin Group (USA) Inc., 375 Hudson Street, New York, New York 10014, U.S.A. • Penguin Group (Canada), 90 Eglinton Avenue East, Suite 700, Toronto, Ontario, Canada M4P 2Y3 (a division of Pearson Penguin Canada Inc.) • Penguin Books Ltd, 80 Strand, London WC2R 0RL, England • Penguin Ireland, 25 St. Stephen's Green, Dublin 2, Ireland (a division of Penguin Books Ltd) • Penguin Books Australia Ltd, 250 Camberwell Road, Camberwell, Victoria 3124, Australia (a division of Pearson Australia Group Pty Ltd) • Penguin Books India Pvt Ltd, 11 Community Centre, Panchsheel Park, New Delhi – 110 017, India • Penguin Group (NZ), 67 Apollo Drive, Rosedale, North Shore 0632, New Zealand (a division of Pearson New Zealand Ltd) • Penguin Books (South Africa) (Pty) Ltd, 24 Sturdee Avenue, Rosebank, Johannesburg 2196, South Africa

Penguin Books Ltd, Registered Offices: 80 Strand, London WC2R 0RL, England

First published in 2009 by Viking Penguin, a member of Penguin Group (USA) Inc.

10 9 8 7 6 5 4 3 2 1

PHOTOGRAPH CREDITS
Insert page 7 (top): Photo Chuck Pulin
Insert page 10: © Chase Roe
Insert page 12 (top): © David Lee 2008
Insert page 13 (bottom): © suekwon
Other insert photographs courtesy of Nelson George

LIBRARY OF CONGRESS CATALOGING IN PUBLICATION DATA
George, Nelson.
City kid : a writer's memoir of ghetto life and post-soul success / by Nelson George.
p. cm.
ISBN 978-0-670-02036-2
1. George, Nelson. 2. Music critics—United States—Biography. 3. Authors, American—20th century—Biography. I. Title.
ML423.G317A3 2009
781.64092—dc22
[B] 2008027422

Printed in the United States of America
Set in Iowan Oldstyle • Designed by Carla Bolte

DEDICATED TO MY FAMILY,

FOR THE LOVE AND THE LESSONS

Between 1950 and 1957 alone, Brooklyn lost a total of 135,000 men, women, and children. They were buying the blarney about the suburbs, they were buying cars, they were moving out to the sticks. Filling the housing vacuum they left behind, 100,000 newcomers moved in, many of them black and Puerto Rican, many also seeking a better tomorrow, as their predecessors had. Another wave of resettlement for Brooklyn.

—Elliot Willenski, *When Brooklyn Was the World: 1920–1957*

CONTENTS

INTRODUCTION

This book is called *City Kid* because, well, quite honestly I couldn't survive in the suburbs or the country. I don't drive. Malls give me hives, and I've never dined in a Denny's and don't wanna start now. This book contains few descriptions of rolling hills, limpid pools of water, or clear blue skies. There is, however, much talk of playground games, nightclubs, and boundless ambition.

Almost the entire book takes place in four of New York's boroughs, with the exception of a chapter in Detroit, two in Los Angeles, and two in the Tidewater area of Virginia. I could have slipped in chapters set in my other favorite cities (London, Paris, Amsterdam), but this book is about how family and art intersect, and the most important connecting points for me are the concrete jungles of America.

Peace.

CITY KID

HOW I CAME TO BE

Like most black Americans, I have only a fleeting understanding of my family's history. I know nothing of my African ancestors, but, thanks to the diligence of a few relatives, I do know a few things about my American ones. My two family trees were rooted in Virginia and North Carolina during the Civil War era. At some point during the early 1860s, in the small town of Bracey, Virginia, just north of North Carolina, Willie Butcher, a black man, met a white woman named Pinkey George. Miscegenation was much more common in this country, and in the South in particular, than our official histories let on. Yet a real romantic relationship between a black man and a white woman in that part of the country at that time makes me think Willie and Pinkey were crazy in love.

This union produced one son, Thomas George, born in 1862. Thomas, who married Harriet Boyd, born June 1, 1864, toiled on the Boyd plantation. Harriet's father, a houseboy on that same plantation, was named Nelson Boyd, and Harriet gave his name to one of their six children, my grandfather Nelson Sterling George.

Nelson Sterling, born January 15, 1892, was a short, fair-skinned man with sharp, piercing eyes, curly hair, and facial features that suggested that Willie Butcher had some Native American blood coursing through his veins. In photographs Nelson Sterling is always very well dressed in nicely tailored suits that were often augmented by a straw hat. Older members of the George family recall that he was quite a storyteller, and that on some Sunday evenings down in Bracey he'd gather up the children and tell ghost stories. My mother says he was a very graceful, handsome man who grayed early, which only enhanced his looks.

My own memories of Nelson Sterling are fleeting. He died in October 1960, when I was just three years old. I remember a gray-haired man in a suit picking me up and holding me up in the air on a trip to Virginia. It must have been in September of that year, since the family held a birthday party in Grandpa's backyard. I was the first George grandchild, and I was named after him, which must have been a great source of pride. My grandmother, Matdora, aka Mattie Clary, was nearly a foot taller than her husband, and about fifteen years younger, and she had a stern demeanor that was reflected in her omnipresent frown. Matdora would outlive her husband by some thirty-six years, and would be a strong, though not always warm, presence in my life.

What I do know of Nelson Sterling and Matdora's life was that the early years were rough. They lived in a little two-room shack down in Bracey, and, as their family expanded to seven kids, some of them would be sent off for a time to live with other relatives, to ease the financial burden. Later most of their offspring ended up relocating to New York and Chicago. In the 1950s, Nelson Sterling and Matdora relocated to Newport News, Virginia, where a massive shipbuilding and dry-dock company, and the naval base it supported, became an employment hub. The Newport News shipyard, which for decades was the world's largest, was built by Collis P.

Huntington, who'd been the driving force behind the first transcontinental railroad. About his Virginia operation Huntington once said, "We shall build good ships here. At a profit—if we can. At a loss—if we must. But always good ships." From World War II through the Korean War, the shipyard boomed, creating hundreds of jobs that, despite the limitations of Southern Jim Crow laws, ended up feeding scores of black families. Because of the shipyard Newport News became a place where a man of African descent could earn an honest wage, buy a house, and have some self-respect. In the cradle of the Confederacy, Newport News was something of a safe haven for black aspirations.

The Georges moved into a big, three-bedroom home, with a piano she loved to play and a big garden where she grew fruit for preserves and gathered the vegetables for her massive Sunday feasts. But all was not smooth in the household of Nelson Sterling and Mattie. He had a child—a girl—outside the marriage, and not with just any woman, but with one of his wife's sisters. While her children eventually came to accept this unexpected sibling, my grandmother was, not surprisingly, reluctant to do so.

When my mother started dating Nelson Elmer, his father, a World War I veteran, was spending most of the week living at a Veterans Administration hospital, where he'd receive treatment for his diabetes, and then come home on the weekends. It seemed an unusual arrangement, and strikes me even more so now (perhaps fallout from his out-of-wedlock "marriage"?).

My father, Nelson Elmer, was in the middle of Matdora's pack and, like his daddy, was on the short side, and had a gift for gab and a persuasive charm. He and his older brother, James, both served in Korea. When Nelson Elmer came back from Korea in the mid-1950s, he began wooing a cutie who didn't live too far away from the George residence. The girl's nickname was Doll.

Arizona Bacchus's family saga goes back to a North Carolina clan known as Brothers. As far as family historians know, there were nine Brothers children, but only one was a boy—Willie—who kept the name alive, as all the girls took on the names of their husbands. My great-grandmother was named Celia Bacchus, which I've been told was the name of a plantation owner of Greek heritage in North Carolina, but that may just be speculation. Celia had three sons, one of whom, Daniel Bacchus, was my grandfather. Daniel was dark, stocky, and muscular, and, when he was young, had long, thick hair that suggested his family had Native American blood as well. In 1929, at age twenty-nine, my great-grandmother Celia moved with her boys to Newport News. I don't know if she was married or not, but I'm assuming not, as no man's name has surfaced.

The Newport News shipyards were a magnet for working men from around the South, and provided decades of employment for the Bacchus side. Daniel worked there; so would Daniel Junior, later called Son; so would one of Daniel's son-in-laws, and several of his grandchildren. Appropriately, Daniel met my grandmother, Berneda Wilkins, who had also been raised in North Carolina, while working in the Newport News shipyards.

His steady income as a chipper at the Newport News shipyard enabled Daniel to buy a house in a nice Negro neighborhood and raise a family of five. The last of those children was a tiny little girl who was almost named Alabama, after an aunt, but instead ended up with the distinctive name "Arizona." In truth, she was so small that when her brother Rudolph first saw her, he exclaimed, "baby doll," and the "Doll" part stuck. At the time Arizona "Doll" Bacchus was born, her oldest sister, Cecelia, was already married, had had children, and was living in a Southern version of public housing known as Newsome Park.

Doll would become all too familiar with Newsome Park after two life-altering tragedies that occurred when she was seven years old. In the summer of 1943 her oldest brother, Son, was riding his bike with little brother Rudolph on the handlebars, and Doll balancing sideways on the bike. When Rudolph tipped forward at a stop, all three Bacchus kids fell to the ground. Somehow a spoke on the front wheel got jammed into the inner thigh of Doll's right leg, digging deep, and scarring her down to the knee. Due to the poor treatment she received at the local hospital, this childhood injury would trouble my mother the rest of her life.

That was bad, but that winter things became terrible. On the night of January 19, 1944, the family celebrated Berneda Bacchus's forty-eighth birthday. My mother remembers it as a fun evening, with all of her family enjoying ice cream and cake in the living room. The next morning she was awakened by the sound of screaming. It was a familiar voice. Her mother was yelling, "Help! I'm on fire!" Smoke poured into her bedroom. In the hallway she, three of her siblings (Son, Frances, and Rudolph), and a boarder, Mary McQueen, found the staircase blocked by smoke and fire. Son jumped out of the second-floor window and then stood on the ground as Rudolph and the women jumped down into his arms. Once on the ground, they turned and witnessed a frightening sight—the charred body of Berneda Bacchus.

The headline in the local newspaper read, "Kerosene Blast Fatal to Woman." The lead paragraph said, "Berneda Bacchus, 48, Negro, wife of Daniel Bacchus of 714 19th Street, was burned to death this morning by the explosion of kerosene she was pouring into her kitchen stove." Firemen had received the alarm at 8:14 A.M. and "found the victim where she had fallen between the porch and the gate. She was dead, but her body was still burning. Dr. Louis Loeb, city physician, said it was the worst case of that type he had ever seen." The firemen found a five-gallon kerosene can with its bottom blasted out. The large can was apparently filled with gas fumes, which ignited when held over the stove. According to the fire department, this type of accident was very typical in the days of kerosene and cast-iron stoves. My mother remembers standing with her brothers and sisters next to my grandmother as she took her last breaths. Ma says she looked up and counted out "One, two, three, four," gazed at her four youngest offspring, and then closed her eyes forever.

My mother went to live in Newsome Park with her oldest sister, Cecelia, her husband, Eugene, aka Cootie, and their three kids—Jackie, Teddy, and Gertrude. She was technically their aunt, but they were all around the same age and grew up more like brothers and sisters.

Cecelia's husband, Cootie, worked at the shipyard, and was, when he was sober, a quiet, hardworking man. But drink put the devil in him, making him bad tempered and abusive toward Cecelia. Despite years of physical harm, she wouldn't let her sons intervene. Ma watched this relationship for years, and though she revered Ceceila and viewed her as a second mother, vowed never to allow herself to be treated that way by a man.

At twelve my mother moved in with her father and his second wife, Viola. The tale of their courtship is told often, and with no affection, by the Bacchus clan. Apparently Viola had been after my grandfather even before Berneda's death, and wooed him immediately afterward. My grandfather was a dapper man and a hard worker who owned his own home—a good catch. Still, it was a shock when he married her just six months after Grandma's burial. It happened so fast that everyone claimed Miss Viola had "worked the roots" on Daniel Bacchus (aka, used witchcraft to win his heart). The tale that's come down to me, from both my mother and her siblings, is that she was a two-faced woman who showed one side to her new husband and another to his kids.

My mother and uncle Rudolph, both of whom lived at home as teenagers, talk about Miss Viola locking away food when Daniel wasn't home, and denying them meals unless he was present. My mother, who continued to suffer greatly from her injured leg, says she would tell the adolescent girl, "You're gonna be a cripple. You'll never walk right again." She'd also make fun of Berneda, taunting my mother by saying, "Your mother wasn't nothing, and you'll be nothing, too."

This psychological abuse wouldn't have amounted to anything if it wasn't for Daniel's attitude. In the many arguments that ensued between his children and his new wife, my grandfather always sided with Viola. My mother suspects that he may have confronted her behind closed doors, but that was no comfort then, when she felt abandoned by her father.

Left without her mother, and with an unresponsive father and busy older siblings, she created imaginary friends. Ella and Joe Bella kept her company, and provided entertaining companionship.

Despite her leg problems, she was a bright student, well liked by her classmates, and had an adorable smile and a big infectious laugh.

Nelson Elmer and James came back from overseas duty in 1956. James loved the discipline of the army life, and saw opportunities in it that didn't yet exist for black men in most other American institutions. So James became a career soldier, staying in the armed forces until he retired as a colonel in the 1980s. His brother Nelson, in contrast, would rise to the rank of sergeant before mustering out and seeking his fortune in civilian life; he was given the nickname Little Nip, because his yellow complexion reminded other soldiers of their Korean adversaries, whom they routinely ridiculed by calling them "Nips" (a racial insult held over from World War II).

As teenagers in Newport News, my mother had become friendly with James, and even fancied him a bit; but when Nelson Elmer came home he chased after her. His timing was great. She had just finished her sophomore year at Virginia Union University and, as much as she wanted to stay in college, her relationship with Viola and her father was deteriorating. Small and feisty, she was determined to make a place for herself in the world, with or without her father's support.

My father and mother started dating in August 1956. By December they were married, and living in a roomy Bedford-Stuyvesant brownstone in Brooklyn with her aunt Alberta and uncle J.T. When she got pregnant in early 1957 they moved into a nicely maintained three-story rental building at 218 New York Avenue in Crown Heights, a block from a big Baptist church on a pretty, tree-lined street. I was born nine months after their marriage, in the fall of 1957, when my father was working at the post office via the GI bill, and my mother was a happy young housewife. Unfortunately, little Nelson Daryle (that's me) missed all the good times and went on to become a statistic.

From 1880 to 1960, United States government census figures tell us that approximately 30 percent of all black children under fourteen lived in homes with only one parent. The number for white American families during that same period was roughly 10 percent, so there is a long-standing difference in these patterns. But what's most significant for me is the consistency in the number of single-parent black households. From Reconstruction through the long years of lynching, and in and out of two world wars, the patterns of single-parent black family life remained stable. The majority of these families were headed by black women, which eventually gave rise to the cliché of the "strong black woman." But that number also means that 70 percent of all black families had both parents present. That was the world my great-grandparents and grandparents, despite whatever personal issues they had, held together in the face of racism, civil inequality, and plain old personal drama.

It is the census figures released in 1960, however, that foreshadowed a grim future.

The percentage of single parent black families in the 1960 census is 32.3, the highest then recorded. Later reports reveal the subsequent family disaster: In 1980, 53 percent, and in 1990, 63 percent of black children under fourteen were being raised by one parent. So my parents' separation, while personally traumatic, was also part of a larger change in black behavior, one that would lead the generations after me to joke "my biological didn't bother" about their absent fathers. When our family splintered in the early sixties, we didn't know we were harbingers of the future, where the idea of black family would be in a state of constant flux and redefinition.

HIGH FIDELITY

I am in the living room of apartment 6C in the Samuel J. Tilden housing projects located in the once Jewish, soon to be black and Puerto Rican, ghetto of Brownsville, Brooklyn. It is 1960. I am four. I am slender, with big round cheeks and long, curly eyelashes that keep getting into my eyes. I stand on my tiptoes in my stocking feet. I wear pajama pants and a small white T-shirt. My small brown fingers clutch the edge of a Motorola high-fidelity stereo, which is made of shiny lacquered wood and has a lemony smell, from the polish my mother applies every Saturday afternoon.

I feel the bass speakers in my stomach. I smell the polish. I feel the music. Looking over the edge, down into the bowels of the hi-fi, I watch the turntable needle roll across the grooves of a seven-inch record with a blue and white label at 45 revolutions per minute. The song is "Please Mr. Postman" by the Marvelettes. The song is on Motown Records, but I don't know that yet. All I know is that the song is about the man who delivers the mail in a light blue uniform, who possesses an amazing set of jingling keys that opens the long row of metal mailboxes in the lobby.

As much as I enjoy "Please Mr. Postman," I'm anxious to hear the next record. Not just because it's Roy Orbison's "Oh, Pretty Woman" (which is the first record I ever asked my mother to buy for me), but because above "Mr. Postman" on the turntable are a slew of seven-inch singles suspended around a fat brown cylinder. Once "Please Mr. Postman" finishes, the needle arm moves away, a single vinyl 45 plops down on the turntable, and the needle returns, catching the groove and sending the "doom-doom-doom-doom-doom" rhythm of "Oh, Pretty Woman" vibrating through my body.

This Motorola stereo was the centerpiece of my family's living room, and our social life. Ma didn't allow my little sister, Andrea, or me in our living room too often, because she didn't want us sitting on her plastic-covered sofa, playing with the rabbit-shaped ash tray, or fingering the dice-shaped cigarette lighter on her glass-and-wood living-room table. But if we were playing records in the early evenings or on weekends (or after school, when she wasn't yet home from work), it was okay.

All through my childhood, from my first consciousness of music into the early seventies, that Motorola was my passport, not simply to records, but to the vast nation outside New York that the music came from. While the black-and-red labels of Atlantic 45s carried a Broadway address, most of the records in her collection came from Memphis (the Stax Records label was pale blue, with a finger-snapping logo) or Detroit (Motown's black and white label had a red star for the Motor City, while Tamla's colors were yellow and brown). As I read the labels of the records Ma brought home, I slowly became familiar with the cities of soul—Philadelphia, Los Angeles, Chicago, and Cincinnati. By the time I was an adolescent, I could identify certain names that recurred in the credits: Curtis Mayfield, Holland-Dozier-Holland, Steve Cropper. Way before I understood what these credits meant, or who these people were, I was already collecting info for the books and articles I had no idea I would eventually write.

My interest in these records stemmed from a desire to better understand my mother's life. My mother was a soul girl: petite and cute as hell, with a nice little figure, and a bright, girlish smile. Arizona Bacchus George, aka Doll, aka Ma, was full of life, and loved to laugh. Though burdened with raising two kids alone in a Brooklyn housing project, she didn't allow herself to become a stranger to fun. Not only was her ever-growing stack of 45s a testament to her love of music and dance, but she regularly held parties in that sacrosanct living room for her girlfriends and their male admirers. Bacardi and Coke flowed. Gin was always available. Every now and then, one of her cooler friends smoked some reefer alongside legal cigarettes like Kools and Parliaments.

My mother's favorite singer was a raw-voiced Georgia boy named Otis Redding, who, I suspect, represented the kind of unbridled passion on record that she sought but found elusive in life. All her favorites were on the gritty, highly emotive side of soul—Aretha, Gladys Knight, Wilson Pickett, and David Ruffin, of the temptin' Temptations (though she liked the smoother Al Green too).

And I can't forget the Godfather of Soul. I remember the time we took a pilgrimage to the Apollo Theater for a matinee show. It was a chilly, overcast day, and my mother and I joined a long line of black folk, as far as I could see, huddled on 125th Street, awaiting entry. Once inside, we sat in the orchestra near the back. I remember elements of the Brown Revue quite distinctly: Pigmeat Markham did his famous "Here Comes the Judge" routine; the Fabulous Flames danced like demons and harmonized like choir boys; the J.B.s, behind the antic introduction of MC Danny Ray, banged out a medley of the great man's hits.

Then Brown himself appeared, a short, dark man with shiny, processed hair who whirled and shuddered and shouted. On the way back to Brooklyn on the A train, I babbled to my mother about the sweaty man who kept tossing the cape off his back and running back to the mike to wail, "Please! Please! Please!"

It was special for me, not because I'd seen James Brown, but because I was too young for so many of the shows my mother attended. Unlike today, when the separation between adult and kid entertainment has been blurred to the detriment of both, soul music was fundamentally music by, about, and for adults. When my ma put on her auburn wig to see Otis Redding at Brooklyn's Brevoort Theater, or her blue eyeliner to watch the Supremes at the Copacabana, it was to experience things so raw and so smooth, they weren't right for a child to see.

Still, I had access to the records and Ma's parties. Like the proverbial fly on the wall, I'd sneak out of the back bedroom I shared with Andrea, and curl around corners to watch the adults do the Watusi, the Hully Gully, the Mashed Potato, and the Boogaloo. I watched as my mother's friends entered the land of a thousand dances and, every so often, I entered that territory too. To justify my presence at the perimeter of Ma's events, I learned a few dances that never failed to amuse inebriated party people.

Despite a career marred by mediocre records and piss-poor management, Jackie Wilson was a soul god whose onstage athleticism and daring rivaled James Brown. The ex–Golden Gloves boxer's signature move was to go from standing up into a deep split, and then, his sharkskin suit spotted with sweat, slide back up again using his powerful leg muscles. I never saw him live, but watched him do this dance on several TV shows, and I was always impressed with how he seemed to defy gravity. For Wilson, this was as much a trademark as his vocal hiccup (a major influence on Michael Jackson) and his dance songs (many of them cowritten by a young Berry Gordy). I'd get in front of grown folks in my jammies and white socks, and do my version of Wilson's split, drawing applause as well as extra Coca-Cola and potato chips.

Soul music wasn't the only kind of culture to which Ma exposed my sister and me. On Saturdays our little family of three would hop on the IRT elevated train at Rockaway Avenue and head west, sometimes to downtown Brooklyn, but usually to Times Square and Midtown Manhattan, for movies or a play. I remember seeing *Mary Poppins* at Radio City and singing the entire song book, from "A Spoonful of Sugar" and "Chim Chim Cher-ee," to the delightful "Supercalifragilisticexpialidocious" all that summer. *Mary Poppins* may seem an odd obsession for a little black boy from Brooklyn, but that's the point, isn't it? Music can pull you out of the box of your location, circumstances, and the particulars of your life for as long as you sing along. As a child, all this music suggested a universe I didn't expect to travel to but could still visit with my ears.

In a side section of that Motorla hi-fi was a space reserved for LPs. In those days my mother didn't buy many of those. LPs were expensive, and often contained more filler than soul food. Aretha Franklin's *I Never Loved a Man* was there. So was Ray Charles's *Modern Sounds in Country & Western Music*. There were a few jazz albums in that slot as well. They stuck out because they weren't purchased by my mother, but by her soon-to-be ex-husband, my often absent father, Nelson Elmer George.

His taste in records very much reflected his world view. Whereas my mother listened to joyous sermons of secular salvation, my father's records were sad, seductive selections from jazzmen, like trumpeter Chet Baker and saxophonist Gene Ammons, soloists who spent their off-the-bandstand lives in thrall to drugs and, perhaps, to the romantic notion of the junkie as artist. This was music of a nocturnal nature for folks "too hip" to participate in the finger popping of soul.

My father saw himself as one of those people. With a GI bill job in the post office lined up, Nelson Elmer could have joined the growing black middle class and guided his little family into a stable nine-to-five lifestyle that would have eventually placed us in a two-story house in Queens or Long Island. Instead my father got addicted. New York City was his narcotic and it made him high, happy, and irresponsible. Bars and barmaids, thin socks and straw hats, numbers spots and craps games were all more attractive to him than diapers and dishwater. In the fall of 1960 I was three, and my mother was pregnant with my sister, and Nelson Elmer was already living out his big city desires, as evidenced by the women's perfume on his shirts and the bags under his eyes.

The Tilden projects are at the far end of Brooklyn, while Nelson Elmer's exciting new life was lived up across 110th Street in Manhattan, on the wide boulevards of Harlem. There he knew Gene Ammons, tried to act as cool as Chet Baker, and remade himself into an uptown cool cat, the kind of man he'd probably wanted to be since boyhood in Newport News. Of course, it took me a long time to learn all this. All I knew was that my father wasn't there, that he liked music without words, and that he had moved to a faraway place called Harlem, which to my little ears sounded like "Holland." Being an early reader, and a careful observer of both Saturday morning cartoons and Dutch Boy paint commercials, I knew Holland as a land of windmills and wooden shoes.

One of my most vivid childhood memories of my father involves the film noir life he'd created for himself uptown. He picked me up from the projects in a long, powder-blue Cadillac with pointy tail-light fins and bright whitewall tires. He wore a jaunty straw hat with a black-and-red band and a matching red-and-black knit sweater. He was a short, yellow, bantam rooster of a man who had a wonderfully phony-sounding laugh that amused him greatly. I always felt he made lots of jokes just so he could luxuriate in his own chuckle. He told me we were on our way to Harlem. When I wondered aloud if we'd see windmills, my comment so tickled him that he repeated it to everyone we'd meet that day. We drove up-town via Riverside Drive, as I craned my neck to get fleeting glimpses of fabled buildings and nameless skyscrapers.

I was still looking for windmills while my father maneuvered into a parking space way east, somewhere in Spanish Harlem. We took the elevator up in a well-maintained apartment building to the residence of a fleshy, fair-skinned woman in a black wig who referred to Nelson Elmer as "Pete Smith." My memory fails me as to whether I'd been prepped for this stunner or not, but either way it was still weird. Most people I knew either called him George, his last name, or Elmer, his middle name. My mother called him Nelson. Pete Smith? This must have been his alter ego, the guy who'd emerged from his cocoon in Harlem.

Why Nelson Elmer George revealed his "other self" to me, and exposed me to a woman I assume was his lover, remains a mystery. Perhaps he was sending a veiled message to my mother. When I got home and related the tale of Pete Smith to Ma, she just laughed and went back to watching television.

After leaving the woman's home, we stopped at a Harlem bar filled with bright neon beer signs, well-dressed patrons, and the stale, sweetly stinky aroma of spilled drinks, Old Spice cologne, and menthol cigarettes. Bluesy jazz, like the Jazz Messengers and Jimmy Smith, flowed from a fat, centrally located jukebox. My father propped me on a bar stool and introduced me to the barmaid, whose name was either Mabel or Thelma or Peaches, or one of those old Negro names that colored people loved and that African Americans have wiped from the phone book.

As she distracted me with a Coca-Cola float (crushed ice, Coca-Cola, and vanilla ice cream, topped with a cherry), my father slipped into a backroom to "do a little business." I presume this was Pete Smith talking. I felt like I sat on that bar stool for an eternity. I watched beefy women slowly roll their hips as they danced with men in snap-brim caps. I watched a machine spew out Kool and Newport cigarettes, and marveled as the multicolored bottles disposed of their contents through metal nipples that regulated the flow of liquor into short, round glasses. In other words, I sat on that bar stool long enough to know I didn't belong in that bar.

When "Pete Smith" returned to retrieve his "little man," I was more than ready to head back to Brooklyn, soul music, and my place in front of Ma's Motorola hi-fi. What I couldn't know then was that much of my adult life would be spent in moody, music-filled rooms just like that bar in Harlem.

THE VILLE

The motto of Brownsville, Brooklyn, when I was growing up there was "I'm from the 'Ville. I never ran and never will." A cool sentiment but far from the reality of my life there. My father ran, and, in doing so, profoundly affected the trajectory of my life. Since boyhood my dealings with my father have been sporadic, short-lived, and not intimate in the ways that matter most. When I was younger that was his fault; as an adult, it's been mine. That we share the same name save the middle one is obviously not our only similarity. When confronted with the unpleasant, emotionally challenging work of (re)building a father-son relationship, I've opted for avoidance over conversation, absence over entanglement.

My mother calls my father "a jack of all trades and a master of none." In his life Nelson Elmer George has been (as far as I know) a postman, a merchant seaman, a short-order cook, a bartender, a taxi driver, a security guard, a process server, and a low-level cocaine dealer. In Nelson Elmer's DNA there's a hustler gene that's been passed on to me. I've had a true nine-to-five job only once in my life and that was only from January 1981 to the spring of '82. In that brief sojourn into the workaday world, I detested the moments in my hole-in-the-wall office, all the while knowing that the world was revolving without me out walking around in it. I've always felt more comfortable as a freelancer, dependent on my wits, smarts, and eyes for opportunities. I may never have been Pete Smith, but I must admit, I understand the impulse.

I sometimes wonder what my life would have been like if I hadn't discovered writing and let it obsess me. I imagine that as a semiskilled, big-city African American male in the latter part of the twentieth century, my life wouldn't have been much different from that of my father. I'd have floated from thing to thing in search of satisfaction, subject to a wanderlust that would have never quite been quenched. Without a marketable skill, I would have scrambled for small checks, and lived off-the-books for decades.

Writing saved me from that naked economic uncertainty. However, it's never made me rich: it's always just gotten me by. For every year of six-figure success I've enjoyed, there have been long periods when I've felt about to be tugged back down into the relative poverty of my childhood. Because I've lived most of my life in Brooklyn, I often find myself on many of the streets where I grew up. Looking around it now makes me all the more aware that my family lived just a few notches above real economic peril.

I was an adolescent, and my sister in single digits, when Nelson Elmer made a rare holiday season appearance at our apartment. The Christmas tree was up, with wrapped gifts and a few toys scattered underneath. Red and green lights were up in the window; and my mother, as always, had many glass and porcelain decorative dishes filled with walnuts and candy. It was a festive room, and we were hopeful that Nelson Elmer was visiting to enhance our holiday. He came into the apartment wearing an out-of-season light-colored suit and pointy-toed Italian loafers. In fact, he brought a few pairs of shoes with him for me: powder blue (like his) and purple, and a couple of other highly impractical colors for a Brooklyn schoolboy. My mother just looked at them, rolling her eyes when he presented them, and laughing when he left.

The centerpiece of his visit, however, was his theatrical presentation of money to his two children. Sitting cross-legged for a time on our plastic-covered sofa, like a visiting potentate, Nelson Elmer placed a stack of bills on the living-room table. Our eyes gravitated to the bills. It was all of our long-delayed child support–Christmas present–guilt money in one delivery. He spoke for a while, talking of getting together more often, etc., and then he left. I walked him to the door, but Andrea, always a practical girl, snatched up the stack of bills as soon as the door closed. She pulled a couple of twenties off the top, but they quickly gave way to tens, fives, and a few singles.

I imagine the idea of sitting there calmly, with the money on the table, must have appealed to his desire to seem important. He must have enjoyed the rush of power he received watching us sit anxiously, wondering how much was there. But it was a con he must have learned uptown. Surely he had to know that as soon as he left we'd see that it was fool's gold. Surely he'd know that we'd be disappointed, that all that theater would just feed our mistrust.

Often as an adult I've tried to put myself in Nelson Elmer's shoes, trying to understand his behavior—not as a disappointed child, but as a black man trying to make it in early sixties New York City. It's a huge leap in context, probably an impossible one. So I've asked a number of older men over the years how someone could become a Nelson Elmer, a man comfortable abandoning his wife and two kids for the streets of Harlem.

I got one memorable answer at a black music convention in Atlanta called Jack the Rapper, a now defunct but once essential gathering place for radio jocks, record executives, and musicians that began loosely in the fifties and ran well into the nineties. At Jack the Rapper you'd meet and greet a cross section of old wise men who knew everything about our music and quite a bit about life.

Perhaps because I hadn't had a father, and hadn't really had a relationship with my grandfathers, I gravitated to the older vets, men usually in their late forties and fifties who passed on knowledge that filled up my articles and books. One night I sat up at a hotel bar with an old record-promotion man who'd been married too many times to count, and was about to hook up with a woman twenty-five years his junior. We started talking about family, and I opened up a bit about mine.

"I understand your bitterness," he said, in his high-pitched, deep South drawl. "But you gotta understand your father probably never felt free a day in his life until he got to New York." The promo man painted me a picture of the South as a landscape dominated by women, noting that "in those small towns you can't make a move without someone seeing you. If you had a secret you could be sure it wouldn't be one forever."

He told me that brothers were constrained by racism when they moved outside black areas, and by social conventions within the black community, especially if they were working men. The promotion man suggested that "when men started moving up North to the bigger cities, it was the first time they could actually be alone. You walk two blocks in New York and no one knows your name, or who your father or mother was, and no one gave a damn really either way unless you could do something for them."

I wanted to dismiss it as a facile explanation, but it did make some sense to me. My father had grown up with a willful mother, an absent father, a sharp-witted younger brother, and five sisters. The Norfolk–Hampton–Newport News axis made for a comfortable, midsized Southern town, but if you didn't want to work for the shipyard you'd have to find your future elsewhere. After the Korean War his brother found freedom in the Army. My father chose New York. As sociology, the promotion man's comments made sense.

When I was born my mother and father were living at 218 New York Avenue, a sturdy brownstone-style rental apartment in Crown Heights, where he was making some side money as a handyman. The owners, an older white couple, were feeling the tug of white flight, and talked about selling the place to my parents. Because he didn't think he could raise the down payment or get a mortgage, my father turned them down. Soon after my sister, Andrea, was born in 1961, we moved from home-owner-dominated Crown Heights to the spanking new Samuel J. Tilden public housing project in Brownsville. Rent for a two-bedroom apartment was only sixty-five dollars a month, with electricity and gas included. Obviously a good deal.

Back then public housing had yet to acquire its rightful tag as "ghettos in the sky," and was seen as a vast improvement over the crumbling, firetrap tenements they replaced in the former Jewish neighborhood. From the 1930s into the 1950s, Brownsville had been a sprawling, working-class ghetto, home to "tough Jews," some of whom founded the notorious Murder Incorporated gang. Remnants of that old neighborhood were visible everywhere.

On the opposite side of the subway tracks from Tilden were soot-and-dirt-covered tenements that had rusty metal fire escapes regularly covered with drying laundry. Garbage cans vied with fire hydrants for sidewalk space. The tenement windows were perpetually open in summer to catch the odd breeze. During the winter, clothes were shoved against window cracks to stop the cold from sliding inside. These tenements were giving way to housing projects in Brownsville—one kind of slum housing giving way to another, turn-of-the-century construction replaced by Kennedy-era visions of urban uplift. These were the places the ghetto Jews of Alfred Kazin's *A Walker in the City* had lived. A few were left on the streets in the Ville, but they were mostly old. Almost all of the younger residents were black and Puerto Rican, recent immigrants from the warmer, softer places. Compared to the tenements that would slowly be "urban renewed" out of existence, these sixteen-story buildings must have looked good.

About four blocks of tenements had been demolished to build the Samuel J. Tilden public housing complex, eight apartment buildings situated next to the IRT elevated subway. Behind and next to Tilden were two more complexes: the Van Dyke projects, which were also sixteen-plus-story buildings, but covered four blocks; and the Brownsville Houses, three blocks of five-story buildings constructed around courtyards. It was amid this mass of public housing that our little family relocated to 315 Livonia Avenue, apartment 6C, of the Tilden projects.

That sense of optimism the project first suggested didn't last the decade. By 1968, when I was eleven years old, I saw a TV documentary that called Brownsville the worst ghetto in the United States. I remember getting a perverse sense of pride from that pronouncement, and I told everybody who'd pay attention about our ranking. If you were gonna live in the ghetto, it might as well be the highest of the low. To this day the Ville remains a deeply entrenched ghetto area, where every urban ill you can think of thrives and change is nowhere in sight.

Most of my early memories of the Tilden projects are sepia-toned and sun-drenched. We played ancient New York City street games handed down from the Jews and the Italians, like the chase-and-catch game ringolevio, where two teams competed to see who could capture the most opponents. It was a fast, frustrating, and often violent game that resulted in ripped shirts, major collisions, and long, inconclusive battles. In its own way ringolevio trained you in the capture-avoidance techniques that would be useful against both cops and robbers.

We also spent hours playing skelly, a game in which clay- or gum-filled bottle tops were knocked, with thumb and pointer finger, across thirteen boxes, and back. This journey was complicated by your opposing players, who either blasted your top far off the board or knocked you into "skelly," a no-man's-land in the center of the thirteen boxes. Once trapped in skelly you had to negotiate with the other players for your freedom, an often painful process, where your self-respect was always up for grabs. In its own way skelly was a playful but pointed lesson in what happens when you allow your fate to be determined by others.

As my friends and I grew older, two sports dominated our days, and often our nights—stickball and basketball—two more games that had filled the streets of Brownsville before blacks and Puerto Ricans arrived. But our version of stickball was very different from the manhole-to-manhole contests associated with Jews, Italians, and the great Willie Mays up in Harlem. We never played in the street, where we'd have to dodge traffic and ice cream trucks.

The Tilden projects contained large concrete play spaces broken up by fenced-in patches of grass, and manufactured play areas, with monkey bars and jungle gyms (skeletal metal structures you could climb onto or swing from) and concrete barrels you could crawl through or climb over. We often used the barrels as a backstop, which kept the balls from bouncing through or over the wire fences, and sent the balls bouncing back toward the pitcher. Any ground ball that wasn't caught was a single. If a batted ball made it on the fly over the nearest fence, it was a double. Over that fence onto the sidewalk, or over the big dirt patch in the middle of the grass, was a triple. Now depending on which direction you played in, a stickball home run had to either hit the side of the farthest building or bounce off the gated windows of the Baptist church that shared our block.

We played with pink Pensy Pinky or Spalding (pronounced "Spaldeen") balls, which tended to turn spongy when hit, so unless a ball was a vicious line drive, it was hard to break windows. Our bats were either regulation baseball bats or, more disposable and thus more popular, used broom handles, or "official" stickball bats purchased at a sporting goods store. One summer some kids raided an ill-guarded warehouse nearby and liberated boxes full of orange broomsticks. They weren't very sturdy, and the cheap paint came off in your hands if you sweated too much, but they were free, and we wore out our supplies that summer.

There was a stickball hierarchy at our end of the projects, and the Puerto Ricans who lived in building 360 were generally recognized as the best players. The black boys, largely from my building,

315, and nearby 305, usually competed against ourselves. Games against the Ricans in the 360 building were serious business, since they took stickball in particular, and baseball in general, to heart. The best player on our end of the projects was Big Red, a left-handed-batting Latino with bright red hair unusual in a Rican. Big Red was renowned for bashing home runs right out of the Tilden projects into the street and, on occasion, over into the Brownsville projects.

I don't recall ever pitching to Big Red, but I have a vivid memory of giving up a stickball homer to the most famous baseball player to come out of the Ville. Though he lived in 360, the Puerto Rican building, remarkably, he was black. We knew him as Mickey Randolph, but by the time he was a star second-baseman with the New York Yankees, he was known to all local sports fans as Willie. He grew up playing stickball on the same patch of concrete as all of us. After becoming an all-city star at Tilden High (we both went to a high school named after the same New York governor as our housing project), Willie was drafted by the Pittsburgh Pirates, an organization then famous for giving blacks and Latinos a fair shot. (In the early seventies the Pirates would be the first major league team to field a nine-man lineup comprised of only black and Hispanic players.)

In those pre–major league years, whenever Willie came home from the minors, it was a major event. Moreover, Willie would still come out, grab a stickball bat, and let us smaller kids try and pump a fastball by him. Somehow I—a lowly figure on the local stickball landscape—managed to get a chance to pitch to him. Wearing my Yankees cap and my favorite red, white, and blue sweatbands, I reared back to fire my seventy-five-mile-per-hour fastball toward the barrel where he waited, with a stickball bat in his brown hands. Willie swung easily and made resounding contact.

As a major leaguer, Willie was strictly a singles and doubles line-drive hitter, but on this early-seventies afternoon, he blasted a tape-measure stickball homer, one that traveled high and deep, smashing the ball against the metal grating above the sixteenth story on the roof of a nearby building. I was proud. To have delivered not simply a homer, but a monstrous shot, made it special. I'm sure Willie has long since forgotten that swing, amid World Series rings, years in Bronx pinstripes, and his appointment as the Mets' first black manager, but I treasure that afternoon as the closest to being a big-league pitcher I'll ever come and, more profoundly, as a testament to an urban street life that'll never be that innocent again.

MY HERO

On one level I experienced the social upheaval of the sixties just like most Americans did—via television. I was a single-digit child most of those indelible ten years, so I was well removed from all the marching and chanting I watched via Walter Cronkite and the evening news. I remember seeing John F. Kennedy's funeral on a black-and-white TV, and watching John-John salute his father's coffin before I went outside to play. I recall the sad night of Dr. King's assassination with only a fleeting understanding of his work. I was transfixed by the violent battles between brutal police and boisterous protesters at the 1968 Democratic convention in Chicago.

Yet the many movements that shaped the sixties and seventies truly rippled down to me through how they affected my mother, her friends, and the other adults I encountered. The most direct impact was that the era's heightened sense of possibility inspired Arizona B. George to change her life.

In 1961 she was a pregnant mother of one, not yet in New York four years, married to a Korean War vet, and living in a ghetto public housing project. My mother was stressed about the marriage during her pregnancy, and things didn't get any better after the arrival of my sister, Andrea Patrice George. Yet when Nelson Elmer began spending less time at his post office job, and more at Harlem bars, Arizona mustered the courage to kick him out. Single black mother with two kids in PJs—we were just a living, breathing statistic from the infamous Moynihan report on dysfunctional black families.

My mother was a small, plucky, determined woman, not unlike one of the characters Cicely Tyson later played in 1970s' made-for-TV movies like *Miss Jane Pittman* and *A Woman Called Moses*, black women who persevered in the face of racism, sexism, and poverty. Her family nickname may have been "Doll" but she wasn't fragile or childlike. In the early sixties Ma juggled and struggled through a series of odd jobs—grocery store clerk, bank teller, seller of Prince Matchabelli perfume at the Abraham & Strauss department store downtown—all the while nurturing the dream of becoming a schoolteacher.

Back then black parents possessed a very conscious memory of the evil efforts made to deny us even the most elementary schooling. Unlike today, when many folks labor under the illusion that hip-hop will feed the black masses, people took the need for education very seriously. For her, becoming a teacher was very much a political act to fight years of institutional racism.

One of the catalysts for pushing my mother from dream to action was my first-grade teacher. She was a middle-aged white woman with a very loud red wig and a disinterested attitude toward her students. It wasn't until after the semester started that the parents were informed that she was just a few months short of retirement, and that she was working only to secure her pension. The lady had mentally retired years beforehand so for the first couple of months, our days were spent writing Xs and Os in block letters in our black-and-white composition books. Furthermore, my class was composed predominantly of black children who were being bused to predominantly white P.S. 189 from Brownsville, so we were being given a grossly inadequate start to our education.

My mother had already taught me how to read simple sentences before kindergarten, so for her to see me writing Xs and Os in the first grade made her mad as hell. She, and other parents, complained, and our teacher upped her activities slightly. Sometime before Christmas our red-wig-wearing instructor left to a hopefully restless retirement and was replaced, to my mother's shock, by a black teacher. Mrs. Harper was a matronly looking woman who wore her hair in a bun, angular glasses, and muted red lipstick. Mrs. Harper had been in the school system for years, primarily as a substitute, and actually lived very close to the school. My mother struck up a friendship with Mrs. Harper that endured.

For a while during the second grade I took piano lessons at Mrs. Harper's house, a lovely brownstone on Eastern Parkway in Crown Heights. It was my first time in such a well-appointed black abode, and I spent more time marveling at the wood floors and floral sofa than practicing my scales. While my mother drank coffee with Mrs. Harper I was supposed to be practicing, but, invariably, I found myself poring through the many copies of the Curious George books Mrs. Harper had collected. I never did master the piano (or anything else musical), but the contact with Mrs. Harper was a tonic for Ma and me.

In the late sixties my mother became a paraprofessional, a kind of teacher's aide, while also taking night classes at Brooklyn College in pursuit of a degree in education. So while righteous brothers and sisters were marching for their rights down South, and angry black folk were rioting for respect up North, my mother was engaged in her own battle for advancement.

She worked all day, came home, cooked dinner, and then either took two buses or two trains out to Flatbush to attend Brooklyn College classes. On school nights she was rarely home before ten. I was responsible for watching over my sister, helping her do her homework, and doing mine. We had to be in bed before eight but often stretched our bedtime so we could catch adult fare on TV, like *Peyton Place*.

Getting into bed was just a formality, anyway. I couldn't sleep until I heard her key enter the door. Often I'd stand by the window and look down Livonia Avenue to the area under the elevated subway tracks, hoping to see Mommy coming home, schoolbooks under her arm, with her eyes peeled for muggers.

We were both anxious and vigilant, with good reason. As Ma pursued her bit of the American dream, Brownsville was growing nastier and more predatory. In the hideous drug culture of the sixties that destroyed lives and, to a great degree, sapped the vigor out of the civil rights movement, a poor neighborhood like Brownsville was ground zero. I gauged the change by the growing danger I felt taking out the garbage.

To get to the garbage disposal I walked down one straight hallway, made a left turn past two elevator doors, two stairway doors, and one window. When we first moved into the projects this had seemed more irritating than dangerous. My first inkling that this wouldn't always be the case came from the glue sniffers. One or two guys would be standing by the window with small bags under their noses, inhaling from open bottles of Elmer's glue till their eyes glazed over. They'd look over their shoulders at me, chuckling at my pajamas and house shoes. Unlike the later drug users of America, the glue sniffers weren't very violent, since their high could be purchased for a dollar alongside a model of the Mercury spaceship.

When heroin flooded the streets in the midsixties, it felt like a shroud fell over Brownsville. Everything got a little darker and more desperate as the glue sniffers gave way to a new kind of drug user—the junkie. Junkies would stand by the corner of Rockaway and Livonia, right by the subway exits Ma took at night, sometimes asking for money, but too often snatching purses, and occasionally taking lives. "Mugging" and "ripped off" entered our urban vocabulary. People were getting beaten up, raped, and murdered all over Brownsville, as heroin escalated the brutality that poverty inspires.

In 315 Livonia, junkies found haven in the stairways and elevators. They'd go into a nod, piss on themselves, and befoul the air. Our mailboxes, little metal coffins drilled into the lobby walls, were regularly either picked or pulled off their hinges. Mailmen became reluctant to come into project buildings. The day welfare checks were due for arrival became a time of high anxiety, as mailboxes, mail carriers, and welfare recipients became targets for addicts and muggers.

But for me, the most psychologically damaging thing the junkies did (often in concert with plain old juvenile delinquents) was to either break or unscrew the lightbulbs on stairway landings. So walking up or down those stairs, you often had to walk up into pitch-black staircases. Obviously the elevators were the best option, though the lights on them could be broken too. The elevators were easily sabotaged if you pressed too many buttons at one time, something any kid could do, much less a determined mugger. Often, a dark stairwell was the only way up.

For years Ma braved the junkies at the train station, the muggers on the streets, and the cretins in the stairway to make a better life for my sister and me. I used to look at the ceiling of the bedroom my sister and I shared and wonder what would happen to us if she was murdered. Who would take us? Perhaps my father's family in the Bronx? Would we be sent down to Virginia to be with my ma's family? Or would we be split up and get lost in an orphanage? Plan for the worst and hope the best—this remains my motto, and it comes from those long nights anticipating my mother's return.

Even as a child I was very aware that our future hung by a slender thread—the ability of our mother to survive the dangers of New York. Her obstacles weren't all external. That injury she suffered as a little girl haunted her many nights in Brooklyn. I'd often walk into her bedroom and see a heating pad on her leg. I tried not to look too hard, because she had horrible scars on the inside of that leg that had never truly healed. On two occasions the swelling in her leg became so severe that she had to be hospitalized. I remember a male family friend carrying her out of our apartment, past our bedroom door, as we watched with moist eyes.

Always, though, she came back home. Past the muggers and away from the doctors, Arizona came home, and we'd survive the latest crisis. For years our family was able to rise above the tide of tragedy that always seemed just outside our door, but not always by very much.

A THIN LINE BETWEEN LOVE AND HATE

There's a picture of my sister and me that sat framed over my fireplace for years. It's a black-and-white, and was taken when I was three or four, and my sister still had only a few teeth in her mouth. The photographer, a balding white man with swatches of hair on either side of his head, set up in the living room and placed a white drop cloth on Ma's Motorola hi-fi. My mother placed me on top of the hi-fi, and then my baby sister next to me. She was a yellow gal, same complexion as her father, and had slightly slanted "Chinese eyes."

Unlike me, Andrea Patrice George was a demonstrative child, with a loud voice and an intense disposition. On that day, though, it didn't take much for the photographer, using funny faces and a big smile, to get our attention. Ma stood next to him, encouraging us both to smile. In the picture Andrea is reacting to the offer of candy, reaching out for it with a palpable sense of joy. I'm smiling too, looking as bright eyed as any happy little boy should. It's the only picture I have of us looking that happy together, and the earliest document of a relationship that would go wrong at some point, and stay wrong for too many years.

I loved Andrea from the moment my mother brought her home. I didn't know until decades later that my father had been very slow in coming to the hospital to see her. It was a big blow in the battle between my parents that was slowly coming to an end. Maybe some of my mother's anger found its way into the womb, because Andrea was willful from the word go, both stubborn and tough, vulnerable and sensitive. Reading her rhythms was never the easiest thing to do.

For some reason, when we first moved into 315 Ma stored all the cereal in floor-level cabinets in the kitchen. Andrea, not satisfied with just having cereal for breakfast, would pull open the cabinets, pry open the boxes, and gleefully spill the Cheerios on the linoleum. Then, laughing, squash the cereal with her hands. When truly inspired, baby Andrea, who was as fascinated with cigarette butts as with cereal, would dump out the ashtray onto the floor, creating a mess of crushed cereal and ground-up ash that drove Ma crazy.

Once the boxes had been shifted to higher cabinets, Andrea moved on to more practical toys, but always with her own peculiar spin on their purposes. I had a Mickey Mouse telephone made of metal, and it had a string cord that connected it to a hard, black receiver. It was all hard edges and rough surfaces, the kind of toy that would never make Toys "R" Us's shelves today.

I loved imitating Ma on the phone. Andrea quickly picked up the habit too, except she had no interest in sharing the toy with me. One day, right around the time of the photo, we were crawling around on the floor, and a battle over the Mickey Mouse phone ensued. I wanted to play with it too, and she wouldn't let me. I pulled at the receiver and, with surprising force and quickness, she slammed me between the eyes, nearly knocking me out. Then Andrea laughed triumphantly.

I've never forgotten the Mickey Mouse battle, not because of the small knot I received, but because I felt it spoke to the dynamic of our childhood relationship. I was the older brother, trying to be in control, and failing, while my sister was bold, had little fear, and was often reckless.

When I was around seven or eight, and just beginning to understand that I was growing up in a tough neighborhood, bullies would try to intimidate me. They'd try to steal my Pensy Pinky rubber ball, cheat me at games, and ask for money. Out of nowhere my little sister would show up and challenge them. "Don't mess with my brother!" she'd demand. After chuckling a bit, they'd either leave me alone or mock me, saying that my sister had more balls than I did. I told her to stop; I could fight my own battles. Sure it was a sign of real love, but it was damned embarrassing, and it made me seem more bookish than I already did in a neighborhood where that was perceived as weakness. Maybe I was just more than a little jealous of her fierceness.

But she could be playful, too. Christmas 1970 is one of my favorite memories of our childhood. We were Jackson 5 fanatics, and for the holiday season Ma had bought us *The Jackson 5 Christmas Album*. Bonded by the Jacksons singing "Little Drummer Boy" and "I Saw Mommy Kissing Santa Claus," we danced around our living room with giddy energy. We were just in the moment together. She didn't try to act cool. I didn't try to boss her around. We were equal in the joy of those records. It was funny, in retrospect, that we both loved "Mommy Kissing Santa Claus" so much because, despite its candy apple cuteness, there was something melancholy about the notion of our single mother getting kissed in our living room.

From the time of her birth until we moved out of Tilden in the midseventies, Andrea and I shared a bedroom, a closet, and a dresser. As a result, our bedroom became a physical and psychological battleground. We had one room and one parent, and that became too much for two siblings to share comfortably. There was an invisible line between the two beds, so toys and clothes had to be placed on the proper side, or yelling and fussing would ensue. Who got more dresser or closet space was a constant battle.

As we got older this forced intimacy grew even more complicated. I began masturbating seriously around age eleven, so I'd have to time my self-pleasing for when I was sure she was sleeping and/or had her body turned away from me. It made an uncomfortable, clandestine activity feel even more risky and embarrassing. Every now and then I'd catch her giggling as she watched from under her covers.

That sense of sexual discomfort cut both ways. I remember a summer afternoon when we were sitting watching television. Suddenly Andrea stood up looking shocked. She made a small animal sound, and then ran into the bathroom. She started calling for our mother, who quickly followed her in. I heard a lot of anxious whispers, but I couldn't make out any words. After a while Ma came out and walked over to me. Her eyes were sparkling and her voice amused. "She just got her period," she whispered, but not quietly enough. Andrea opened the door to yell in a rage, "Don't tell him!" She was angry at Ma for betraying her sudden secret, and at me for the undoubtedly silly smirk on my face.

Ma finally got us out of the projects when we were both adolescents, liberating us from the tensions of sharing a room. I had mine and she had hers. But that necessary change exacerbated the growing distance between us. The days spent conversing, much less playing or dancing, together had ended. Even how Andrea achieved in school differed from how I did—while I was a reading/writing maven, Andrea excelled at math. We had a classic left brain/right brain split.

By the time I was a teenager I sometimes experienced nostalgia for the days when Andrea had followed me around. That big brother/little sister affection had been replaced by indifference or downright hostility. I remember a particularly nasty argument in the kitchen over something, and it started getting physical. I grabbed her and tossed her to the ground for stepping to me with way too much attitude. I was much taller and stronger, so as far as I was concerned, she could fuss all she wanted, but she wasn't gonna swing at me and get away with it.

Vengefully, Andrea pulled a knife out of a cabinet and came at me with it. I sprinted to my room and closed the door, as I heard the knife bounce off the wood. We fought often, but this knife incident was a new low. Sometimes I wasn't sure if she cared if I lived or died, and that made me sad when I wasn't thinking of kicking her ass. Her favorite song when we were kids was the soul ballad "Thin Line Between Love and Hate," by the Persuasions, and for too many years my sister and I lived out this melancholy title.

PEER PRESSURE

As a child, my interest in reading greatly fueled my erotic imagination. My mother was a big reader of pop pulp fiction: Ian Fleming's James Bond series, *Valley of the Dolls*, *Peyton Place*, *The Carpetbaggers*. By nine I was already a voracious reader, and I'd sneak into her bedroom to check them out. I soon figured out that there were code words on a page that meant sex scene: "bosom," "loins," and, my favorite, "vulva." When I saw them on a page I'd stop skimming and slow down.

These words were often modified and amplified by "heaving," "inflamed," "engorged," and "sensitive." Any combination of these words meant characters were having sex. I got so good that within ten minutes of opening one of Ma's paperbacks I had identified two or three scenes. It would be my pleasure afterward to show these passages to my friends, displaying both my reading skills and growing sexual sophistication.

Like a lot of city kids I lost my virginity on summer vacation. Either in July or August Ma would ship Andrea and me off to Virginia for a couple of weeks, where we'd shuttle back and forth between Grandma George, Uncle Son, and Aunt Frances. We usually had the most fun at Frances's place, since she ran the loosest house, had fun kids (cousins Becky, Chubby, and Quinton), and was the most dynamic character. Aunt Frances was a big-boned brown woman, with wide hips, a hearty laugh, and a passion for beer, bid whist, and men.

Neighborhood kids circulated through Aunt Frances's house all day. It was there that I met a local gal I'll call Tammi. I was about eleven, and she was maybe three years older. Like a lot of Virginia gals, Tammi was what we called "healthy"—wide hips and a butt that undulated when she walked. Back then I was frequently complimented for having curly eyelashes, and Tammi found them quite cute, along with my New York accent.

One afternoon, in a neighbor's toolshed, she let me fondle her beautiful brown breasts, which started a stirring down below. I was in that phase of boyish adolescence when just the sight of a sexy woman got me uncontrollably excited, so the feeling of sucking Tammi's breasts was just unbelievable. I didn't really know what to do after that. Tammi did. She pulled down her pants and panties and lay on the floor. She unbuckled my Lee jeans. I remember how we wiggled about the toolshed floor, my knees against the concrete floor, the smell of gasoline from cans in the shed, and the sounds of kids running in the distance.

Back in Brownsville I bragged about my lost virginity to all the brothers on the basketball court. While it gave me some respect, it had still happened down South (everybody "got some" down South). When was I gonna have a Brownsville girlfriend? That's when Cynthia came into my life. She was a butterscotch fourteen-year-old cutie known around the Tilden projects for her shiny black bangs and neon-blue coat. To the amazement of many suitors, she picked me to be her first boyfriend.

One day Frankie, a Puerto Rican buddy of mine who lived on the third floor of 315, arranged a meeting between Cynthia and me at a nearby school yard. By the time we'd walked the three blocks home we were holding hands. Because she lived in 305 and I across the parking lot at 315, we could sit in our kitchens looking at each other as we talked on the phone. My first relationship made me giddy and proud, like I had some heretofore unknown value. My self-esteem skyrocketed, but my confidence was neither deep nor strong.

You see, my boys greeted my first romance with snickers. After a touch football game a couple of guys said they'd been walking with her in the rain. "So," one kid I never did like said, "I had to pull out my rubbers." To the delight of everybody but me, he pulled out a pack of Trojans. In retrospect, I think he did it as much to show everyone he had some as to humiliate me. But this incident, plus the constant barrage of my friends' cherry-popping tales, caused me to blow it with Cynthia.

One afternoon I found myself miraculously alone for a few hours in 6C. I got Cynthia to come over. I pulled the curtains shut in the living room, screwed in the red lightbulb Ma used for parties, and put on an Al Green record. I laid down the law: "We need to start having sex." Cynthia's exit line from my den of seduction was devastating: "I thought you were different."

Only after the fact did I realize that Cynthia had approached me precisely because she perceived me to be a nice, cute, nice, book-reading boy, and not one of the wannabe fly guys that filled the Ville. I was probably what Cynthia wanted, and, if I'd just been who I was for her, good things would have come my way eventually. Yet in Brownsville circa 1973 (and to this day), it was hard to embrace non–Super Fly aspirations. So, like the sad dude in the Chi-Lites' "Have You Seen Her," I sat by the kitchen window watching for signs of Cynthia, trying to figure out how to balance what the local culture demanded versus who I was.

A THEATER ON PITKIN AVENUE

Pitkin Avenue in Brownsville was a thriving commercial shopping strip that had been pioneered by the Jewish merchants to serve the Hebrew families that had once populated the neighborhood. When I was a little boy many of the stores still bore Jewish names, and even the more generic-sounding businesses (Thom McAn's, Woolworth's, East New York Savings Bank) were largely run by folks with Jewish surnames. But by the midsixties stores began to close, as their old clients split for other Brooklyn neighborhoods like Canarsie, to the suburbs of Long Island, or to the hurricane corridors of Florida. Often they were fleeing my family and the others like us who were turning Brownsville black. The bonds blacks and Jews had shared during the glory days of the civil rights movement broke down in neighborhoods like Brownsville where Semite merchant and black customer now eyed each other with mutual suspicion.

Sometimes blacks, Puerto Ricans, or Arabs took over the stores. More often, however, these places either shut down or were burned down, leaving holes on Pitkin that wouldn't get filled for decades. You couldn't totally blame them. Heroin had turned rough streets mean. Purse snatching, shoplifting, muggings, and armed robbery abounded in and around Pitkin. The phrase "ripped off" entered the vocabulary as a verb for crime. I used to put my money in my sock whenever I had to go over there. It made for smelly but somewhat safe dollar bills.

One oasis from the change was the Olympic Theater, located at the far end of Pitkin, just a block or two before the avenue melted into Eastern Parkway. To get there from the Tilden projects you could take a bus up Rockaway Avenue, passing the Brownsville projects, a church, cheap furniture stores, the fish markets of Belmont Avenue, and on up to Pitkin. At Pitkin you then transferred to another bus for the long ride past its stores and vendors. Or, if you were like me, trying to hold onto every slim dime, you walked up to Pitkin and then across it to the Olympic.

The Olympic was a high-domed, ornate movie palace whose lineage went back to vaudeville, and certainly smelled like it. As a symbol of Pitkin's decay, the smell of the venerable entertainment venue lingers. First it was just the mildew in the restrooms. As the theater evolved from a cross-cultural meeting place into a Saturday playground for the dark children of the projects, the stink spread. With time the scarlet carpet turned crimson with ground-in dirt. Broken seats proliferated. Ticket prices rose. The stink rose to high heaven.

I remember clearly seeing two movies at the Olympic, both of which got me thinking about race relations. In 1964 I went with my mother to see *Zulu*, a celebration of British imperialism whose set piece depicted a gallant regiment of redcoats trapped in a crumbling compound as a mad tribe of Zulu attacked and attacked and attacked. The good old boys from the Merseyside were valorous, dying in gritty, noble close-ups. They lined up in disciplined lines. They fired, reloaded, and fired into waves of brown- and black-skinned Zulus who in broad daylight served themselves up as cannon fodder. Except for close-ups of the scowling Zulu king, Shaka, the Africans were photographed in a distant, impersonal manner. The Zulus were bodies; the British soldiers had faces.

As a child, I very much wanted to root for the folks who looked like me. But the film's visual strategy left little room for anything but the mildest racial identification. Leaving the afternoon matinee you best believe the kids were not imitating the Zulus' tactic of running headlong into gunfire, but those redcoated Brits pulling triggers under a bloody sun. Though blue was my favorite color, I remember getting a red baseball cap just so I could connect with the cinematic heroism of that valiant company. After all, the Zulu may have been brown skinned, but they were African, and I was a Negro.

Or was I a monkey? Negro or monkey seemed to be the options presented by *Planet of the Apes*, which I saw at the Olympic with some friends when I was ten. We planted ourselves in the back row, popcorn piled as high as we could afford, and watched Charlton Heston, truly the white man's white man, try to make sense of a world where the master race were slaves and the monkeys were running things.

Since a typical Brownsville insult was "You a monkey-faced motherfucker," the idea of a world controlled by primates who treated whitey like crap raised a number of interesting questions. If you accepted being called a monkey, by friend or foe, was *Planet of the Apes* a vindication? If you didn't accept being called a monkey and remained a Negro, did the film mean you wouldn't exist in the future, since Negroes were scarce (a black astronaut arrived from the past with Heston but was quickly stuffed and mounted by the apes as an artifact of a bygone era). If you identified with the apes because your nose or forehead betrayed some simian origins, did that mean you felt the desire to enslave whites? Finally, if you did identify with the apes, did you dare tell your friends?

I didn't think all of this when I was ten, but the questions buzzed around in my head for years after seeing *Planet*. This kind of socio-political mulling was a big reason there were so many sequels to the original film. *Planet* was so sixties in its concerns, so smart about race and power, that the civil rights movement, nationalism, and every other "ism" of the time could be contained in its sci-fi universe.

My fellow ticket holders in the Olympic made it clear what side they were on by yelling for the apes to lobotomize Heston. Many were pleasantly surprised when, at the film's end, a fractured Statue of Liberty was stuck in the sand, to Heston's horror. There was a general "that's what these fools deserve" feeling as we all exited out into Pitkin. Maybe if some brothers and sisters had been alive during the film, my neighbors would have cut Heston some slack. But Hollywood didn't give black folks love, so we didn't need to give any either.

Looking back, the funny thing to me is still Heston. The "no gun control," neocon stud, who'd played that most Jewish of Jews, Moses, in *The Ten Commandments*, was the last white man left. The significance of Heston in that role sure wasn't lost on the filmmakers and publicity flacks. But all I knew for sure was that Heston didn't look a bit like any of the remaining Jewish merchants on Pitkin Avenue.

Sidney Poitier, though born in Miami, was reared in the Bahamas, and he arrived in New York in 1943 with nothing but a thick accent and great ambition. I didn't know Sidney was from the Caribbean when I watched his work as a kid, which was good, since it would have made me view him negatively. Before Bob Marley and Rastafarianism put an Afrocentric, rootsy spin on Caribbean culture, I'd always viewed its transplanted natives (an upper-crust merchant class had been settled in Brooklyn for years) as snobby, snotty, and uppity. They had houses, first in Bed-Stuy and Crown Heights, and later in Flatlands, East Flatbush, and Flatbush proper. I went to school with their kids. I visited their neat little homes. I felt the odd condescending tone in adult voices. I sensed that they felt it was a shame I lived in the projects and my parents were from "down South," and not Trinidad, Barbados, or Jamaica. My last name was George (a typical last name of colonized folk), but my domestic pedigree made me suspect, even if they thought I was "a bright boy."

Sidney, whose career was built on masquerading as an African American, successfully avoided our prejudices. The very qualities I admired in Sidney were the things that made me resent the Caribbean folks I knew. The funny thing is that the regal bearing he projected would, in another context, have seemed insufferably superior. The most sympathetic thing about Rod Steiger's redneck sheriff in *In the Heat of the Night* was that the poor guy had to grapple with Sir Sid at his most lordly. It's one of the few parts where Poitier's haughtiness often overcomes his natural charm, resulting in one of his deepest characterizations.

Even in the wilting southern heat the second button on his suit always stayed closed. Anger flashed across his face when he slapped a racist Southern patriarch, and when he shouted, "I'm a police officer!" at Steiger's bewildered sheriff. But flash was all he did.

Righteously angry, yes, but never so consumed by it that he was reckless or stupid. To see an entitled black man projected on a huge movie screen was an amazing thing in 1967. My mother made sure I experienced Poitier as much as possible. During his amazing run in 1967 of *In the Heat of the Night; To Sir, with Love;* and *Guess Who's Coming to Dinner*, we saw them all. At ten years old I was given a crash course in sepia-toned white-collar masculinity. Because of his character, intelligence, and confidence, Sidney Poitier became the man I wanted to be. If he existed, even if it was just onscreen, I could, maybe for a moment, maybe just when I needed to, be Sidney Poitier. For a boy without a father, Sidney became a very useful role model.

SOUL SONGS

Every morning in the sixties my family woke up to WLIB's *Soul at Sunrise,* a broadcast hosted by the mellow and melodious Eddie O'Jay, a baritone by way of Cleveland and, yes, the vocal group was named after him. The title *Soul at Sunrise* was no corny phrase either—it was accurate. LIB had one of those funky sunrise-to-sunset licenses most black stations at the end of the AM dial were saddled with, so O'Jay's show started both our days and LIB's.

Every school day started with syncopated organ accompanied by drums. Eddie's voice was low and slightly raspy, with precise elocution that sounded as good selling Nu Nile hair grease as it did introducing Shorty Long's "Function at the Junction." O'Jay had a rhythm-and-blues voice that prodded but didn't push you out of bed. His voice let you catch another minute or so under the covers before you reluctantly gave in to the necessity of washing up, eating breakfast, and taking a rowdy bus ride to school. So for years our radio was set at 1190 on the AM dial.

There were secrets on *Soul at Sunrise* that it took me years to decipher. O'Jay would announce "BYOBB" parties for the coming weekend. Took me a while to get someone to tell me that meant "bring your own brown bag," aka no alcohol was served but you could bring your own, a reflection of the fact that many black-oriented clubs didn't have a liquor license.

Another sample of O'Jay's shows were ads for the Boston Road Ballroom, a magical uptown nightspot I never got to visit, that every few months housed the *Jewel Box Revue*. Again it took me into my adolescence to find out that the *Jewel Box Revue* was a touring troupe of female impersonators. It was weird to me that "punks" and "faggots" were so reviled by the adults around me, yet people would pay money to see men dressed up as women.

By the time I was old enough to figure out what the Jewel Box was, LIB was being replaced at our home by technology. The black owners of LIB purchased a station on the FM band and called it BLS, which, in the Black Power–influenced early seventies, was known as the "black liberation station," though it ultimately liberated only our listening habits, which ended up being more than enough. Out was the AM static at the end of the dial and the restrictions of daylight broadcasting. In was full-bodied sound twenty-four hours a day. Now we were experiencing the lush colors of music made by Curtis Mayfield, Gamble and Huff, and Barry White. Where LIB had been gritty and kinda country in its on-air style, BLS embodied the upwardly mobile class consciousness of college-educated blacks and those with white-collar aspirations.

WBLS's morning man was Ken "Spider" Webb, an avuncular brother with the demeanor of a suburban father gathering up his sleepyhead kids. No ads for the Boston Road Ballroom, the *Jewel Box Revue*, or Nu Nile hair grease on BLS. Webb would announce "the color of the day," and scores of black New Yorkers would dig out their green slacks or black sweaters or yellow socks to match Webb's request. Sometimes you'd be on the bus or subway to school, and you'd spot black folk sporting Webb's colors, and found yourself part of a warm, connected family of listeners.

While Webb set a family tone in the morning, it was Frankie "Hollywood" Crocker, the afternoon-drive-time jock, who truly defined the station. In terms of cultural impact in New York City, Crocker was to the seventies what Jay-Z later became at the turn of the century—a style icon and an arbiter of cool. As the city's top-rated afternoon DJ, BLS's program director, and New York's leading black concert promoter, Crocker's musical selections helped define New York taste for many. Crocker's voice was a luscious, low tenor, well matched to a smooth, glib delivery and a suave arrogance that allowed him to say, "If I'm not on your radio, your radio isn't on," and pull it off.

Reed thin, with a well-maintained Afro (that evolved into curls and a perm as the decade progressed), Crocker was a certifiable Big Apple sex symbol, who once celebrated his birthday by riding into Studio 54 on a white horse. In the early seventies the station's slogan was "The total black experience in sound," and it very much was that with a wide range of nonsingles-driven artists, like Jon Lucien, Marlena Shaw, and Grover Washington Jr., who he featured alongside Stevie Wonder, Earth, Wind, and Fire, and the Ohio Players.

But as BLS's reach grew, so did its ambitions. Could a black station redefine its identity and capture the pop market? By the time I was in college BLS was calling its format "urban contemporary" and its slogan became "the world's best-looking sound." Crocker expanded the playlist to include the Rolling Stones ("Miss You"), Queen ("Another One Bites the Dust"), and all the disco you could stand—Silver Convention ("Fly, Robin, Fly"), Cerrone

("Supernature"), Salsoul Orchestra ("Brazil"), and more. Crocker was living a crossover life, and the station reflected this. For a while this programming strategy worked, making BLS the city's number-one station, the first time a black-owned broadcaster had earned that distinction. Black radio had traveled a very long way from WLIB.

Despite the black community's collective pride in this success, as a young listener I felt increasingly that the station's playlist was missing something. Funk bands that were huge within the national black community (Cameo, Con Funk Shun, the Bar-Kays) and a slew of still vital deep soul survivors (Bobby Womack, Candi Staton, Millie Jackson) either didn't get played at BLS or only got played if they made "disco"-sounding records. And without Crocker's support they rarely got booked to play clubs, much less concerts, in New York. Moreover, not only did I miss what I wasn't hearing, I actively disliked much of what Crocker played, feeling that in building its ratings BLS had turned away from the black community that LIB and early BLS programming had embodied.

Over time my personal discomfort with BLS's direction evolved into a sense of betrayal that fired me up to write about music. By the time I was attending college I had come to believe that the musical (and social) values I'd grown up with were being replaced by music that was plastic and robotic. Looking back, I see that it was a profound desire to conserve the old soul music values that drove my interest in music criticism. The thing that saved me from being just another critic using the past to beat up on the present (the jazz world is full of them on and off the bandstand) is my curiosity. I loved Otis Redding like an uncle (and he was more a presence in my house growing up than any of my real uncles), but my taste never calcified.

For example, I knew Luther Vandross was special the first time I heard him sing with a studio group called Change. You can't find two singers from the same soul tradition more different in vocal quality, approach, and demeanor than Otis Redding and Luther Vandross. And yet both spoke to me and, on more than one occasion, made me tear up and cry. They wrote songs that communicated deep emotion—just as R. Kelly does today (in his rare lucid, nonobscene moments).

There's a space where tradition and innovation coexist, where to revere the past is not to close your ears off to the present. Trying to find artists who did both, and studying how they did it, was a central theme of my life well before I was writing for a living. In retrospect, reconciling the revolution in radio from LIB to BLS, from AM to FM, from the rooted sounds of soul to the upscale ambitions of eighties pop, has been an obsession of mine since the mornings of *Soul at Sunrise*.

HANGING WITH CAPTAIN AMERICA

In the sixties I, like scores of future writers, was a member of the Merry Marvel Marching Society. I still have the oversized button I received for my membership fee featuring the comic book faces of Captain America, the Hulk, the Thing, and Spider-Man. In the Tilden projects I was not alone in my allegiance to the Marvel Universe. Along with my three best friends, Junior Williams (a lanky jock with a house full of family), Gary Smith (a stocky West Indian who could hit a stickball pitch a mile), and Dan Parks (a skinny, horn-rims-wearing bookworm like myself), I assiduously collected Marvel's superhero soap operas every week with my allowance money. All of us lived in 315 Livonia, and would travel in a pack down to the newsstands by the Rockaway subway station to pick up the latest installments.

It was Marvel, by the way, and almost exclusively Marvel. D.C. Comics never held my interest for any length of time. I'd look at Batman and Superman from time to time. Maybe sample the Green Lantern or the Justice League, but the D.C. format, in which evil was dispatched at the end of each issue, seemed way too easy. It didn't pull you along the way Marvel's stories did, and none of the D.C. comic heroes, save the odd Batman story, had the complexity of Marvel's many tortured souls.

As a budding student of history I gravitated to Captain America, not because I felt particularly patriotic, but 'cause I loved the World War II backstory, and his unending jousting with the Red Skull, a Nazi villain who, like Captain America, had somehow survived the war (and the decades) in fine fighting shape. That Captain America was endlessly tortured by the death of his protégé, Bucky Barnes, resonated with me as well. In Cap's angst over the loss of Barnes, I projected some of my feelings about my absent father. That could be the adult me grasping for significance, but there had to be some reason I chose Captain America's dilemma as my own, instead of Spider-Man's troubled love for Mary Jane, Iron Man's fragile heart, or the Hulk's uncontrollable fury.

Any homoerotic yearnings in Captain America's constant moaning for Bucky went well over my head. Back in the Ville when I was growing up, if you were a punk or a faggot, you were castigated as effeminate or womanly. Captain America was an ass-kicking hero. There's no way he loved Bucky in any way other than fellowship. Yet when I look back at those many issues where Cap mooned over his young charge (and never had a real love interest from World War II to the sixties), it all does seem a bit queer now.

Anyway, I followed Cap in his own comic as well as in the Avengers, where a collective of superheroes gathered at Tony Stark's palatial Manhattan mansion (Stark being Iron Man's secret identity) to meet, train, battle intergalactic evil, and balance their outsized egos with the unending job of saving the Earth from destruction. Captain America was the only Avenger without some super or plain old special powers: Thor was the mythological god of thunder; Hawkeye was the world's greatest archer; Iron Man was cloaked in a computerized suit of hi-tech armor, etc. All old Cap had were some amazing reflexes and a red, white, and blue shield with a star in the middle. He was the Avenger's most mortal hero, and I one very mortal fan.

Junior, Gary, Dan, and I purchased our comic books at one of three newsstands/candy stores located in the shadow of the Rockaway Avenue elevated subway station. They were probably originally owned by Jews, serving the population that dominated Brownsville before public housing. By the sixties they were manned by Arabs. They could have been Egyptian, Syrian, or from Iraq, but those niceties of Middle Eastern ethnicity were beyond us. All we knew was that they were swarthy, pronounced English with an accent, and were quite clannish in that they rarely employed folks from the surrounding community.

The comics were racked in neat rows along the walls opposite the cashier, right alongside *True Confessions*, *Reader's Digest*, *Bronze Thrills*, and other pulpy pastime reading. It was at these newsstands that my allegiance to the moral code of Captain America was sorely tested. As the price of comics rose from ten cents, when I started collecting, to twelve and fifteen cents, the pressure on my weekly allowance increased.

So did the peer pressure to shoplift. Over time the comic collectors in Tilden developed a number of techniques. The more advanced could roll a comic into cylinder and slide it up their sleeve, either next to their arm or around it. The more typical move was to slide it flat against their stomach and right down their pants, flipping their shirt over their ill-gotten booty. At various times all my friends copped a comic or two, saving twenty-four cents that could be used toward a Mr. Softee cone or baseball cards.

I'd been afraid to shoplift, afraid of being caught fleeing across Rockaway Avenue to the safety of the projects across the street, of being arrested and, even worse, forced to face my mother's disappointment. But one day money was low, and the new Captain America was out, and a major battle with the Red Skull was under way. So at the urging of my friends, and propelled by my desire, I stood with two friends as we all slid one or two comics down into our Lee jeans. We were spotted by one of the Arab dudes behind the counter and made a mad dash for the exit, dodging people buying newspapers, kids with candy, and slow-walking pedestrians. I was well out into the middle of the street when I heard one of the Arab guys yell, "Hey, you stop!" and, as if grabbed by my shoulders, I jerked still.

My friends kept going, reaching the block of our projects, while I froze, and then turned to face the young shopkeeper, quietly handing over Captain America. I was really at his mercy. He could have had me arrested, or called my mother, or both. Instead he simply took the comic book from me, leaving me in the middle of Rockaway Avenue to stew in my embarrassment and the ridicule of my friends, clutching their "free" comics and laughing. Clearly crime was not a career option.

Comic books were also our link to the rapidly disappearing white families of the Tilden projects. When we first moved in, there were whites sprinkled throughout all the buildings. The public housing authority, apparently sensitive to the race question, clearly had put more Puerto Ricans, blacks, and whites in certain buildings, in some effort to create a community, I guess. There was a white family right next door to us in 1961. But as the sixties moved on, they began to flee.

The last white family I knew of lived at the end of the projects, down by Rockaway Avenue. The son had a sweet comics collection, and I remember Junior and me going to visit him to offer some in trade. I remember him cracking open the door suspiciously, though we'd seen him at the candy store many times. He had dirty blond hair and a milky white complexion. We'd heard some rumor that he'd been beaten up recently, though I saw no evidence of it on his face. But clearly he wasn't interested in trading, he wasn't going to let us in, and he sure wasn't coming out. Within weeks he, his family, and his comic books were gone. That kid was the last white boy I remember living in the Tilden projects.

We all took great pride in our collections, which were usually stored in discarded milk crates or cardboard boxes that had contained canned foods at the local supermarket. Junior was fanatical about *Spider-Man* and *X-Men*, and kept his comics in pristine condition, like he knew that one day they'd be worth real money. The man had copies of early editions of his favorites, which he kept in plastic bags. My collection was never that choice or well maintained, partly due to having to squeeze them in a closet crammed with my sister's and my toys and clothes. But, to be honest, while I loved the comics (and all my other stuff), neatness never counted much to me.

On the weekends, when we didn't have our heads in comic books, we went looking for fun outside the neighborhood. Together the four of us, along with whoever else had carfare, would hop the train at Rockaway Avenue and ride to the Deuce (aka, Forty Deuce, aka Times Square, aka Forty-second Street), to the strip of theaters between Seventh and Eighth avenues, an hour-plus ride, where we'd compare notes on fly-ass *Soul Train* dancers and relate the latest tale of a mother being mugged on a stairwell. The deeper into Manhattan the "iron horse" rode (our nickname for the subway), the fewer black faces came aboard. Four loud, boisterous black boys drew anxious glances and steely glares from other riders.

We'd emerge from the subterranean station into Forty-second Street's urban blightscape: the tawdry glow of crumbling old theaters; noisy-clanging-beeping pinball arcades; greasy luncheonettes; and cheap-looking hookers. But that didn't faze us, 'cause we had an appointment to meet with the kings of Forty-second Street. Their names loomed large on the marquees of the Harris, the Selwyn, the Amsterdam, and the other movie houses of the Deuce. After paying $3.50 we'd pay homage to the only black superheroes we knew (outside of the Black Panther): Richard "Shaft" Roundtree, Fred "the Hammer" Williamson, Jim "Slaughter" Brown, Jim "Black Belt" Kelly, and, of course, the queen, Pam "Coffy" Grier.

From the sticky floors of the orchestra or a smelly balcony, we spent the afternoon cheering car chases, ogling busty women in distress, and savoring dialogue laced with "fools," "suckas," and "muthafuckas." In their multicolored bell-bottoms and two-toned platform shoes, they wore threads that freed them to live as large and insolently as we all dreamed of being one day.

Underscoring the cursing and the revenge-fixated plots were the chicken scratch of guitars, the percolating polyrhythms of congas and bongos, and the wailing of soul singers about "a bad brother" ready to "take down the man." Sometimes, when the movie was really bad (as in "not good") and the scent of cheeba induced a contact high, I'd close my eyes and let the great soundtracks of that era fill me up. After the credits rolled, it was back onto the Deuce for hot dogs at Nedick's on the corner of Forty-second and Seventh Avenue (where Shaft ate) before we boarded the train back to Brooklyn. On the way home we'd reenact our favorite scenes, quote choice dialogue, and hope we'd have enough money for carfare and another movie next Saturday.

This mix of comics and blaxploitation movies (later augmented by Bruce Lee and kung fu flicks) was, along with sports, the fuel for our daydreams. Perhaps because Dan and I were the least athletically gifted of the quartet, we ended up extending our fantasy lives longer than Junior and Gary. I remember we had an ongoing game in which we were astronauts in outer space who encountered a beautiful Russian cosmonaut on a regular basis. I've forgotten her name now, but she was our space-age love interest for a couple of summers.

As we grew older I stayed closer to Dan than I did to Junior and Gary. I still have these great pictures of us at Junior's in downtown Brooklyn, munching pickles in our good suits the day we graduated from P.S. 189. But we went to different junior high schools, and grew apart bit by bit. Moreover, Dan, perhaps because he was always being picked on in the Ville, felt freer to step outside the cultural boxes we then all lived in.

While we were all grooving to the Temptations' "Psychedelic Shack" and Al Green ballads, Dan started sporting a bandana, and he put a Jimi Hendrix poster over his bed. He was listening to "Purple Haze" back when no one around the way knew who Jimi was. No self-respecting black music head today wouldn't anoint Hendrix a god, yet in the early seventies the conventional wisdom was that he played "white-boy music," that Jimi had no relevance to "black is beautiful," or to the funky grooves rocked at neighborhood house parties. Dan, however, stuck to his guns. Embracing Hendrix in a black ghetto circa the early seventies was raising your freak flag high. It was stating that you were an individual and didn't give a damn who judged you.

Still, the real shocker was yet to come. One afternoon Dan came up from the fifth floor and knocked on my door. It was after school, so I was working on my homework, glad to be distracted. We sat down in the living room, and I put on some 45s and listened as Dan told me he was a "gay," which was a relatively new term in the lexicon of sexuality, but I quickly figured out what he meant.

His tone was downcast and subdued, as if he knew this would change our relationship, but he didn't shy away from the consequences. It was really brave of Dan to tell me this. I know that now. I didn't then. My mind leaped back to all the times we'd hung out, to our years of friendship, and then forward to the present, fearing that for years Dan had been secretly lusting after me.

Not long afterward, Gary's family moved out of the Tilden projects, and Junior started dating a Jehovah's Witness girl he'd later marry. Childhood was over. But Dan's confession (or realization) took a natural evolution and pushed the ending into hyperdrive. I spoke to him after that afternoon, but not very often, and not for very long. I don't know what happened to my comic book collection. I believe my mother did what mothers have always done and, at some point, tossed them out when I was at school. Even before that I had started giving them away, keeping a bare minimum, so that when they finally disappeared I didn't really care enough to complain. All I know for sure is, as with Dan, one day I stopped hanging out with Captain America.

BK '69

On a humid summer day in 1969 I sat in the cafeteria of Brooklyn's Alexander Hamilton High School as James Brown's "Get Up (I Feel Like Being A) Sex Machine" flowed out of several transistor radios. I watched a girl with Afro puffs dance with a lanky dude in a red mesh tank top and Lee jeans. As Brown rapped, "Get uppa! Get on up! Get uppa! Get on up!" I sipped the last drop of milk from my pint carton and got up to go to my last class of the hot day.

I wasn't in summer school, but was participating in one of the lingering Great Society programs from Lyndon Johnson's presidency. It was called Model Cities, and it enabled "at-risk kids" (meaning someone black and young from the projects) to get paid a stipend for attending economic enrichment classes. Model Cities was on its last legs in the first term of Richard Nixon, doomed by GOP budget slashing and wasteful administrators, and, as the dancing in the cafeteria suggests, not everyone in the program was diligent about his scholarship.

In its defense I offer this: That hot day helped change one black boy's life for the better. In an airless, mostly empty classroom our instructor, a soul brother in his mid-twenties with a bushy Afro and a mustache to match, sat on the edge of his desk and held up the *New York Post*, the *New York Times*, and the *Daily News*. Back then the *Post* was a liberal newspaper with a great sports section, the *Daily News* was a tabloid with the best funny papers and a policy of reporting a Negro felony every Sunday on page five, and the *Times* was a huge, unwieldy contraption that was rarely available at ghetto candy stands.

My hip instructor did a very simple yet profound thing: He read the accounts of a single bank robbery as it was reported in all three New York dailies. In the *Times* the crime was buried inside in a single column, and was told in the "who, what, where, when" tradition of objective journalism. In the *Post* the story was near the front, and was highlighted with a bold black headline. In the *Daily News* it was on the bottom of page three, with a thick, blocky headline, a racy subhead, and a lead that was in a larger type than the rest of the article. As I remember, the *Daily News* story had fewer facts than the *Times* or the *Post*, but did seem more lively than the other, more sedate, reports.

By pointing out the political ideology that underscored each paper's editorial policy, this smart soul brother gave me my first lesson in media literacy. I was already interested in writing, but I had never heard anyone break down the many ways in which information was shaped by media bias. I remember that lesson like it happened yesterday—and it informs my thinking to this day. Thank you, President Johnson.

AFRODISIACS

As a single cutie who loved music and parties, my mother met many men in the sixties and seventies. Black cops in particular seemed to like her. She dated two that I remember: an uptight light-skinned dude named Arnold, who was the first black in his precinct, and was intensely conflicted about his job; and Ben, a big, brown, easygoing gent, who used to stop by our house for bowls of soup on winters' nights when he was supposed to be patrolling Brownsville's mean streets.

Not all the men who stopped by apartment 6C were boyfriends. Post–Nelson Elmer, Ma built a network of relationships with men who became surrogate big brothers, men she could count on, who became role models for me and possible boyfriends for her girlfriends. In the midsixties she befriended a group of groovy guys called the Afrodisiacs 3, who promoted parties. They were all tall, lean, cool as the other side of the pillow, and wore shades as comfortably as tigers wear stripes.

One of the crew was named Gary. He had a radio DJ deep voice, bedroom eyes, and a luxuriously laid-back manner. Every other word out of his mouth seemed to be "groovy," "outta sight," or some other sixties slang. He had one of the first Mustangs to hit the streets, a sleek white beauty he drove with his seat pulled back so far it reached his rear tires. I would have wanted to grow up to be Gary, if his boy E.M., aka Eddie Sawyer, wasn't around.

If Gary was cool like Bill Cosby's Scotty on *I Spy*, then Eddie Sawyer was a more chilled-out Sidney Poitier. He drove a light-colored Volkswagen Beetle when that car was new to U.S. streets. As an insurance claims adjuster, Eddie wore dark suits, bright white shirts, and razor-sharp ties, and carried an attaché case filled with papers, expensive pens, and a Polaroid camera. Walking up to 315 Livonia, Eddie looked like he'd just been cast as the sepia 007. I really don't remember Eddie's eyes since, in my memory, day or night, inside or out, they were perpetually covered by green-tinted shades.

If Eddie's demeanor wasn't already cool enough, his selection of women was always incredible. I remember them always being superfine ladies in hot pants, with long black legs; stylish women, either red boned or dark ebony, with bright orange Diana Ross wigs and frosty blue eyeliner. Eddie had custody of his three daughters by an early marriage but, with the aid of his mother, lived a bachelor's life that I envied as a child, and tried unsuccessfully to emulate as a man.

I loved all his women, but none made a bigger impression than Charles. I recall her as a Halle Berry look-alike, with short hair, pretty brown eyes, and skin as smooth as melted butter. She was the first attractive adult woman to tell me I was cute. She'd come over and hug me, and look at me with those brown eyes, and I'd blush bright red. To me Charles was a woman to have, and Eddie was a role model to be inspired by.

Aside from parties, Eddie had two other defining leisure-time activities. One was smoking reefer, as any cool sixties cat of his pedigree would. The other was hunting. In his bedroom dresser drawers he kept a couple of hunting rifles that, on several occasions when Ma wasn't looking, he showed off to me. One day, he promised, when I got bigger, he'd let me go upstate and hunt with him and his friends. It was an invitation I never got a chance to accept.

The cool world of the Afrodisiacs ended one bloody late-sixties night. Apparently Eddie and Charles were high, perhaps off something stronger than reefer, and for some reason Eddie pulled out one of his rifles. A playful struggle ensued. The gun went off. Charles was shot dead. It was an ugly, drug-fueled tragedy. We all cried because of Charles's death, and then cried some more at Eddie's fate. The shooting was ruled an accidental death, not homicide, which was fortunate. What was so sad was that drug possession charges got Eddie sentenced to seven years in an upstate prison.

I was about ten years old when this tragedy occurred. To this day I think that what happened to Charles and Eddie made me leery of drugs. Though I'd develop a taste for beer and various alcoholic beverages over the years, I always indulged with moderation when I wasn't abstaining altogether. As for herb, I'd be a late bloomer, and a nonparticipant when it came to what folks in the sixties called "hard drugs."

By the time Eddie had been convicted another man had entered my family's life, one who'd be the great love of my mother's life. Stan wasn't the most imposing man I'd ever met. He was coffee colored, with a thick beard, and he was balding prematurely, despite being several years younger than Ma when they hooked up. Unlike the Afrodisiacs posse, Stan wasn't fly. He was an elementary school teacher who Ma met at work, and who, like her, had become an educator to "make a difference in the community," a quaint sixties notion that bonded them as co-workers and lovers.

Ma's cooler male friends thought Stan was square, but Andrea and I loved the fact he was so solid. From my years in elementary school until I started college, Stan was my mother's boyfriend and the stable male presence my family craved. We'd go to Coney Island on Friday nights to get shrimps at Nathan's and ride the Wonder Wheel. We saw movies together and shared popcorn with him. He had breakfast with us and Chinese food dinners. He would bring over the Black Panthers' newspaper and explain to me the difference between a cultural nationalist and a Marxist.

Stan loved sports like I did and took me to many basketball, baseball, and football games. We even saw some sports history together. His father had Jets tickets. So, because of him, I was at Shea Stadium the snowy December Sunday afternoon in 1973 that O. J. Simpson surpassed two thousand yards in a season. (I still have the ticket stubs.)

It was Stan who, at an upstate New York resort, showed me the proper way to shoot a layup on a gorgeous summer day. For a Brooklyn boy it was a gift that keeps on giving. It seems like a small thing, I guess, but for me it was the kind of fatherly experience I'd been starving for. The rhythm of it—dribble, step, dribble, dribble, right leg bend, left leg straight, right arm up—was a dance I still do happily, and Stan was my instructor.

I wish there was some drama to relate about Stan and my ma during the sixties and early seventies. I just remember my mother being romantically content. It allowed her to be consumed by her other dreams—a master's degree, a car, a house. Marriage was always in the air, hovering just a few years off in the future.

JOINING THE LITERARY GUILD

I was about fourteen when I saw an ad in *Esquire* magazine or the *Atlantic Monthly* (I always read well above my age) telling me I could join something called the Literary Guild for one dollar. The offer was a generous four books for a buck. Borrowing books my mother had purchased for her Brooklyn College studies, I'd already read the greatest hits of urban lit—Richard Wright's *Black Boy* and *Native Son,* James Baldwin's *The Fire Next Time,* Claude Brown's *Manchild in the Promised Land,* and Piri Thomas's *Down These Mean Streets.* Plus Ma was a lover of commercial fiction, so I'd read several James Bond novels and books by Jackie Susann, like *Valley of the Dolls.*

What was so seductive about the Literary Guild offer was not simply that I could get four books for a buck, but that if I was clever, those four books could become fourteen. According to the *Esquire* ad, you could order three Ernest Hemingway novels (*The Sun Also Rises, A Farewell to Arms, For Whom the Bell Tolls*), four F. Scott Fitzgerald (*This Side of Paradise, The Great Gatsby, The Last Tycoon, Tender Is the Night*), four William Faulkner (*Sanctuary, The Sound and the Fury, Light in August, As I Lay Dying*), and two Thomas Wolfe (*Look Homeward, Angel; You Can't Go Home Again*) for that single dollar. I'd read some short stories from this bunch in anthologies (Faulkner's "The Bear," Hemingway's "The Snows of Kilimanjaro" and "The Killers," Fitzgerald's "The Diamond as Big as the Ritz"), but was aware of them more as legends than as actual writers.

I figured that this was my chance to start my own, very adult library, without seriously endangering my allowance. So I clipped out the ad, inserted one dollar in an envelope, and hoped I'd soon be not just well read, but informed about literary history.

The box came one morning with a buzz, as the mailman couldn't fit anything that big in our box. I was out playing ball, employing my two moves (a low-trajectory Kareem Abdul-Jabbar sky hook, and a drop-step spin move I stole from Dave Cowens) as I led my three-man squad to decisive defeats. But my substandard game was forgotten once I opened that Literary Guild box. Inside were four sets of books, each color coded: Wolfe's two were thick and sky blue with silver embossing; Faulkner's were red with yellow letters; Fitzgerald's pale blue with black spines; and Hemingway's a dusky blue with white letters.

For a while I just fondled them, touching the covers gently, rubbing fingers over the lettering, and smelling the pages, deriving a strange pleasure from the ink on the page and the pulpy paper used in these editions. Then I got nervous. Was I really mature enough to understand these books, or were they just symbols of my ambition and nothing more? The serious writing I'd read before had been about "the black experience"—meaning our ongoing struggles against racism. But I'd have no easy way of identifying with these writers, who were all white, and all dead to boot.

I began with *Gatsby*. Not for any deep literary reason—just because there was talk of a movie, and I liked to be as on top of things as a child of the ghetto could be (I remember making sure I read *The Godfather* before seeing that flick). I believe it was my first time reading a book that was better than any movie. Whereas the Bond movies were all more fun than Ian Fleming's books, and Coppola's film was art compared to Mario Puzo's pulp, Fitzgerald's book was a sensational read, with his liquid, flowing sentences pulling me along.

I totally identified with Nick Carraway. His cool observations and vaguely condescending, ultimately sad tone really touched a nerve. Even at fourteen I knew that Nick was me. I already had the sense of feeling slightly outside of things happening around me, even feeling outside of things happening *to* me. Sometimes it felt like I was standing next to myself. I always felt I was taking notes on a life I should have been living, and, to me, that was Nick's curse, too.

I didn't really connect with *Gatsby* until I was a young adult. Still, even as a pimply preteen, I could understand Gatsby's desire for reinvention in pursuit of love. I wanted muscles, but stayed a string bean. I wanted to be a shot caller, but was really a bricklayer. I wanted to be made smarter by my reading, but I could barely add higher than 2 + 2. The scene that still kills me is when Gatsby goes down in flames in a steamy Manhattan hotel room, trying to get Daisy to proclaim her love in front of her boorish, unfaithful husband, Tom Buchanan. I remember thinking that no matter how much you try to remake yourself, class differences could be difficult to overcome even in supposedly "classless" America.

I've never cried for Gatsby, but I've come back to his character numerous times, seeing as an adult that his frustrated yearning for an unattainable woman is an apt metaphor for trying to rise in American society. I've met countless black Gatsbys, men obsessed with acceptance, who thought the "right" woman—be she light, bright, and bourgie or white with a pedigree—is as essential as the right bachelor degree to their crossover dreams.

Not as imposing, but still quite pleasurable, was *This Side of Paradise*, Fitzgerald's first novel. Its details now escape me, except for the air of romantic yearning for adventure that hovers over the book, and that young men like me will always be susceptible to.

My attempts at Wolfe and Faulkner were much less fulfilling. I found Wolfe's overblown verbiage boring. I dipped into both of his massive novels and nearly drowned in pages of worthless adjectives. I decided to postpone reading more Wolfe for another time, one that's never come.

My relationship with Faulkner was more complicated. Despite all the references to his greatness in all the literary criticism I read, the man's white Mississippi pedigree and Southern milieu was a turnoff. I knew race was an obsession for him, but I really wasn't that interested in an alcoholic white man's view of "the question." I knew (at least, according to the great critic Alfred Kazin, whom I'd been reading to better understand my Literary Guild selections) that Faulkner shouldn't be viewed (or, at least, solely viewed) through the prism of politics. So with all that in my young mind, I cracked open *The Sound and the Fury* and was confronted with the limitations of my fourteen-year-old imagination.

The shifting point of view and subtle narrative line was just too much for me to grasp. Armed with only my ambitions as a reader and a couple of books on American letters as a guide, I bailed on Faulkner and have returned in dibs and dabs over the years, obviously a major failing in my literary self-education.

I was only one out of three with my Literary Guild authors when my life changed and a love affair began. Like scores before me and,

I hope, many generations after, I found a personal guru in Ernest Hemingway. In that summer I turned fifteen, and then in so many sweet summers since, Hemingway's elemental elegance and hard-boiled humanism spoke to me as style and attitude. I devoured *The Sun Also Rises* and then *A Farewell to Arms*, fixating on the details of fishing, bullfighting, ordering in European cafés, and driving through the Swiss Alps.

Though not as pristine as his classic short stories, in terms of how Hemingway squeezed every ounce of meaning possible out of "and" and "but," these novels were like cool, clear water that reflected back and quenched my thirst. Over the years I'd come under the sway of many artists, but none as artistically ambitious, stylistically influential, and creatively accomplished as Big Papa. (Speaking of big men, whenever I hear the Notorious B.I.G.'s "Warning," with its economical storytelling and matter-of-fact violence, I think of Hemingway.)

Sex was a huge attraction for me in both *Sun* and *Arms*. I never did quite understand what was physically wrong with Jake Barnes in *Sun*. Did his dick get blown off, or his testicles? I mean, could the guy go to the bathroom? The hot-blooded object of his desire, Lady Brett Ashley, tried to roust him a couple of times, only to frustrate them both. This ambiguity was, of course, central to its charm. At the time I only had a vague notion that there was a malady called impotence (at that age I got an erection just walking past a pretty girl). If I found out what Jake had, could I catch it? I'd read the passages dealing with the injury over and over, ultimately trying to decode the tragedy as a preventive measure.

Without a doubt, the central conceit of *Arms*—that a wounded soldier could win the heart of his nurse—was a ripe adolescent dream. War heroism rewarded with sensual compassion is a male romantic fantasy. Only its bittersweet ending redeems the story. That the protagonists of both *Sun* and *Arms* were injured, yet noble and still virile, spoke to me, even though I was as healthy as the next horny adolescent.

The incredible sense of inadequacy and vulnerability kids feel, that overwhelming anxiety that they can't measure up—in school, in sports, with girls—can seem, and often be, as mentally unbalancing as an injury to the body. At least an injury can heal. I spent much of my adolescence wondering if I would ever measure up. Reading about Hemingway in biographies, I came to understand that that adolescent insecurity had lingered with him, both fueling his art and wrecking his relationships.

Hemingway's magnum opus, *For Whom the Bell Tolls*, written with epic intentions and on the full belly of international celebrity in the 1930s, doesn't have the same confused, romantic yearning at its core, and suffers because of it. This tale of a professional terrorist (as we'd call Robert Jordan now) was closer to Hemingway's persona than his personality. I savored Jordan's righteous heroism, and his boning of the coltish Maria, but Bell didn't move me in the ways Hemingway's more callow, less self-assured men did.

On the heels of all of this reading, Fitzgerald and Hemingway became heroes of mine. The irony being that if I'd encountered either man, it's likely that they would have seen me as a potential shoe-shine boy. Black folks were a fleeting and none too dignified presence in their work. *Gatsby* features Nick Carraway's notorious sighting of a "ridiculous Negro" driving in a fancy car on a Sunday afternoon in Manhattan. Hemingway was quite comfortable with the word "nigger" whenever a black man showed up in the background of one of his stories. Basically, black people were irrelevant to them, which, in retrospect, I believe played a part in their appeal for me.

Through my socially conscious, dashiki-wearing, school-teaching mother I'd sampled the books "for black boys looking for images of themselves." Sadly, like food that is good for you, those books interested but didn't excite me. I was all too aware that they were supposed to be "good for me." Filled with ghetto drama, racist whites, and short money, neither *Manchild* nor *Black Boy* nor any of the others hit with the shock of the new like Hemingway or Fitzgerald. To employ a phrase whites once typically used to describe their fascination with black music, I found this white literature "exotic."

So the lack of blacks, especially since the authors were clearly uncomfortable with them when they showed up, didn't upset or offend me. I wasn't seeking role models in their work. I desired excitement, surprise, and literary style. I did read them for social history as well as literary pleasure, but not as empowering sociology. (Only later, as an adult writer, did I come back to many of my mother's books, particular the work of Richard Wright, whose struggles off the page I find quite moving now.)

I was hooked on Hemingway (and, to a lesser degree, Fitzgerald) like one of the marlins Papa hunted off the coast of Cuba, and began to read all I could by and about him. Carlos Baker's big biography (considered definitive at the time) became a trusted friend, and I looked into A. E. Hotchner's kiss-ass memoir too. At this point I was a fan, excited by my entry into a book world so different from the world of fleeing Jews and migrating blacks I lived in. But it wasn't until I started on Hemingway's Nick Adams stories that I crossed the line from consumer to chronicler, from reader to writer.

Nick Adams—young Hemingway—was sprinkled throughout his brilliant first collection of short fiction, *In Our Time*, and Hemingway came back to him again in *Winner Takes Nothing* before anthologizing all the stories in one stand-alone volume. Nick evolved from the young son of a Michigan doctor to a runaway hobo to a soldier over the course of these stories, each one a spare, allusive, pristine example of the writer's art. In the rhythms of Hemingway's prose, and the careful detailing of Nick's existence, I began to formulate the idea that I could write about my life in a similar style.

And so, that summer, after dipping and diving into classic American literature, I got pulled by a profound tidal wave of ambition and decided to write my own story. Hemingway gave me license to see the details of my life as significant: summer baseball, my absent father, my lust, my interaction with white folks, my interest in history. From first adolescent encounters with Hemingway until beginning college at age eighteen, I penned about sixty pieces centered around a surrogate named Dwayne Robinson (my mother almost gave me the middle name Dwayne, though she settled on Daryle, so it seemed an apt dual identity). Some were simply Hemingway knockoffs, others were stylistically more ambitious sketches of moments in my day.

A ritual evolved, especially on weekends, holidays, and those long, hot New York summers, during which I escaped by creating ultraromantic visions of myself. I'd buy little notebooks—mostly small spiral numbers with replaceable pages—and I'd fill them with my attempts at short stories and narrative essays. I'd sit up all night scribbling, and then commandeer my mother's manual (later electric) typewriter and fill the pages with my musings. My mother and sister both have memories of me tapping away until one and two in the A.M.

Occasionally I'd try to write standing up, as Hemingway reportedly did, but my legs were no match for Papa's. I even tried writing while drunk, or at least a little tipsy, like my great alcoholic heroes. Thankfully, I was always a sober sort, so the relationship between inebriation and creativity escaped me, particularly since what I wrote under the influence was crap.

Mostly, I was intoxicated by my own words. I didn't show them to many folks—only some to my mother, English teachers, and girls I hoped to make girlfriends. Mainly I just reveled in their creation, watching the pages of Dwayne Robinson stories grow, hoping they'd amount to something grand one day despite their flaws. Years later I'd name the lead character in my first novel, *Urban Romance*, Dwayne Robinson, and I tossed in a bit of one of those adolescent stories. I would also use Dwayne Robinson as my credit on a cheesy TV movie I rewrote, a joke that I richly enjoyed.

Ultimately, the most important thing wasn't Dwayne but that I'd found a calling. One afternoon that summer I came home and ripped down all the posters of baseball players I had taped up. Down went the Yankees' centerfielder, Bobby Murcer. I'd followed Murcer's career since he first joined the club and was touted as the next Mickey Mantle. He'd never be that, but Murcer was a solid major league ballplayer, one of the first whose career I'd followed from the day he'd gotten called up until he retired. It was tough to take Murcer off the wall, but down he came.

The pictures from *Sports Illustrated* and the *Daily News* that had covered my walls were replaced with photos from *Rolling Stone*, *Es-*

quire, and book jackets. Up went a shot of Eldridge Cleaver smoking a pipe with the Eiffel Tower in the background. Up went a photo of James Baldwin from the novel *If Beale Street Could Talk*, and Jimmy Breslin from his book about Watergate, and Hemingway from a literary magazine, and any other writers I could find. I was acknowledging that my baseball dreams, while not yet completely over, were no longer my chief focus. I was going to be a writer, an idea that would have sounded absurd if I hadn't sent that one dollar to the Literary Guild.

BK EARLY SEVENTIES

When I was an adolescent the uniforms of the New York Knicks were filled by secular gods (Walt "Clyde" Frazier, Willis Reed, Dave DeBusschere, Bill Bradley, Dick Barnett, Earl "the Pearl" Monroe) and in order to keep up with the team in the long, dark ages before cable, all of New York listened to the broadcast announcer Marvelous Marv Albert. His voice was always nasal, but was higher pitched back then. His delivery was as sharp-witted and as sarcastic as only a real Brooklyn native's could be. In the corridors of East Flatbush's Meyer Levin Junior High school Marv Albert imitators were legion. Bruce Gelman and I, both of class 7-14, were just two of the thousands battling to be the best Marv Albert, while using our pens as mikes as we walked the staircases of JHS 285.

"Frazier brings it up the right sideline," I'd say. "He passes to Bradley, who takes two dribbles and feeds into Reed in the post. Back out to DeBusschere. Over to Bradley. He stops. He pops. Yes!"

Then my dark-haired friend would reply, "Frazier at the top of the key. Passes to DeBusschere. He's trapped in the corner. Passes back out to Frazier, who dribbles left, stops, fakes, and then bounce pass to DeBusshere, who lays it up and in!"

The only championships this franchise has ever won occurred

while I was in junior high and then high school, back in 1970 and 1973. Combine these with the titles won by the Mets and Jets at Shea Stadium in '69, and these were amazing years to be young, love sports, and be alive in New York City.

These glory years coincided with my attending two schools in East Flatbush, Meyer Levin Junior High and Tilden High School, which were separated from each other by a narrow street. With my teenage years came my first awareness that race and class were intertwined, and that in Brooklyn, whether a neighborhood was black, Puerto Rican, or Jewish was just a matter of what point in history you walked its streets. It wasn't until I attended Meyer Levin that I found out that Brownsville, just a twenty-minute bus ride away, had a history that predated the projects and the brown folks who lived there now.

One afternoon in a Meyer Levin hallway, I got into a conversation with a white mother who was volunteering in the principal's office, who said she too had grown up in Brownsville. She knew all about the fish market on Belmont Avenue. She knew about the elevated subway that ran down Livonia Avenue. She knew about the Brownsville Boys' Club and Abe Stark Philanthropic summer day camp that was run there.

But what really tripped me out was how she pronounced Pitkin Avenue. Everybody I knew in the projects said "Pick-in" as if the "T" was silent and the street was a metaphor for selecting items, which felt apt, since it was Brownsville's main shopping strip. The lady said "Pit-kin," with a heavy emphasis on the "T" and "kin," which, technically speaking, was the correct way to say it, yet it felt foreign, and, coming from her middle-aged self, sounded old-fashioned.

It was my first inkling that my Brownsville, a place of public housing, of bodegas and brown-skinned peoples, had housed others. Until then we—blacks and Ricans—seemed to exist in our own world, in areas that were a bus ride, a long subway trek, or a goodly car ride away from the Jews and Italians who shared Brooklyn with us. I'd already figured out that my home city was a place of enclaves marked by invisible lines of ethnic demarcation, and that wrong turns carried risks.

But what the woman hipped me to was that this geography wasn't stable. In fact, not only was it mutable, but it was changing all around me. In my Brooklyn circa the 1970s there were the predominantly black and Latin 'hoods of Brownsville, Crown Heights, and Bedford-Stuyvesant; the Italian and Jewish areas of Flatlands, Canarsie, and Flatbush; and the rapidly growing Caribbean population of East Flatbush. Downtown Brooklyn was the land of movie theaters, the huge Abraham & Strauss department store, and Saturday afternoon Chinese food with Ma and my sister. Throughout my adolescence and teen years, blacks and Ricans and the white ethnic areas were in transition, as wealthier whites fled the borough in reaction to us angry brown hordes. Busing was definitely one of the engines of change, but not always the yellow kind.

It took two city buses to get from Brownsville to Meyer Levin, and later Samuel J. Tilden High School. My magic carpet was my precious school bus pass, a wallet-sized card that granted free admittance to subways and buses. Public transportation meant I didn't have to suffer the ignominy of exiting a school bus, but everyone knew where we were from anyway. After all, we came on the same city buses, knew each other, and, most noticeably, were usually all shoved into the same classes. It was possible at Meyer

Levin to travel from darker Brownsville to predominantly white ethnic East Flatbush and yet have only fleeting classroom contact with your white schoolmates.

When I entered junior high in 1969, Canarsie, East Flatbush, and Flatlands were overwhelmingly peopled with white Italians and Jews. By the time I graduated from high school in 1975, all that was ancient history. In fact, I believe, my senior class at Tilden was the last predominantly white one in the school's history.

My personal journey was a little different from that of a lot of my Brownsville peers. Back in elementary school I'd been a star, partly because I was painfully well behaved, was as well spoken as my role model, Sir Sidney Poitier, and because I could read my ass off, which was greatly valued by teachers and administrators. Unfortunately, my reading ability overshadowed my many weaknesses—I had a speech impediment (despite therapy I still mumble), and couldn't do math to save my life. I think reading was so easy and so much fun that I didn't apply myself to math with any seriousness.

When I got to Meyer Levin my reading scores from elementary school landed me in class 7-14, which was an elite group. And, within a few weeks, I knew I was in over my head. A crucial part of my failure was that in the fall of 1969 there was a long, bitter teachers' strike over community control of local school boards.

It's little remembered now, yet it was a seminal moment in New York's racial history. Ground zero for the strike was about ten blocks away from the Tilden projects in an area known as Ocean Hill–Brownsville.

"Decentralization" was an educational buzzword of the period, with the idea that local school boards, reflecting the will of the community surrounding the school, would be able to fire teachers and principals without having to go through the traditional review process. The Ocean Hill–Brownsville school board had aggressively exercised its powers, and the United Federation of Teachers head, Albert Shanker, a combative man who never bit his tongue, saw this as an attack on the seniority system he'd fought hard to set up.

Quickly the battle between the black school board and the white, largely Jewish teachers' leadership became a flash point for the city's black and white tensions. My mother experienced the conflict firsthand. As a young teacher she refused to make black and Latino students recite the Pledge of Allegiance. A white assistant principal tried to get her suspended, and a garbage can was tossed through the windshield of his car by a local activist. "Leave Arizona George alone" was the message. And he did. It's just one example of the black versus white turf wars that infected the school system. The strike ended, but the antagonism between the black community and the UFT (and white New York) continued to fester.

When school resumed in October my class moved at an accelerated speed to make up time. Maybe if I hadn't missed those introductory weeks I might have been able to keep up. But as we moved through algebra and Spanish, I found myself spending increasing amounts of time staring out of the window with the Temptations' "Cloud Nine" playing on my internal radio.

It didn't help my growing insecurity that my classmates were overwhelmingly white, Jewish, and seemingly hugely better prepared for the leap to junior high educationally and socially. Nor was I comforted by the presence of our homeroom teacher, a taciturn man who had a perpetual smirk on his face and Moe Howard hair, who didn't seem to like me very much, or as much as I was used to. As the "black boy who could read," I had gotten lots of attention back at P.S. 189. It wasn't until Meyer Levin that I realized how much that support had meant to me.

I had many memorable interactions that sad year in seventh grade. Of course, there was Bruce Gelman and our Marv Albert–Knicks broadcaster competition. There was Chucky, a tall, curly-headed classmate who called me *"shvarts"* to my face or shouted "Hey *shvarts*!" at me in the hallways. When I asked what it meant, Chucky would say "brother" or "black person." None of my fellow Jewish classmates thought it worthwhile to inform me it could also be used to mean "nigger." So wherever you are, Chucky, I send out a big "fuck you!"

Then there was Brian, a laid-back, passive kid who, along with me, had failed at all the more popular instruments. After failing at trumpet, violin, and flute, Brian and I wound up as the band's baritone section (the baritone horn looks like a tuba, sounds like trombone, and has the presence of neither) and furiously rehearsed our four-bar solo at the Meyer Levin semester-end concert.

My schoolwork also wasn't helped one bit by my full-on discovery of masturbation. I must have glazed all my underwear and pajama pants with semen during those first fanatic months of full-on self-pleasure. Every week *Jet* magazine had some big-hipped sista in a swimsuit in its photo section ("Brenda is a student, aspiring airline stewardess and enjoys go-go dancing. This Macon, Georgia, beauty is 34-28-38"). Then there was *Players* magazine ("for me who is"), the first true black men's magazine. The photo reproductions could be poor, and the girls a very mixed bag, but hey, I wasn't really that picky. My mother endured washing my stained clothes with nary a comment to me. It must be an unspoken rule of motherhood never to mention masturbation to their sons.

Suddenly feeling inferior and helplessly horny, I was dropped down to class 8-8 for the eighth grade, a mediocre status that more truly reflected my place in Meyer Levin's educational universe. Socially I was much more comfortable, of course—more black males, more brothers and sisters from the Ville, though I felt embarrassed when I encountered my former 7-14 classmates in the hallways or cafeteria. It turned out that that feeling of inferiority was good for me. Not being "special" anymore made me bear down on the books. I could still read at a higher level than my classmates, but now, with a real sense of purpose, I applied myself much more to math. No whiz, but at least now I competed.

So for my last year at Meyer Levin I was promoted to 9-12, one of the top classes in my grade. My yo-yo junior high career established a lifelong pattern. I tend to stumble and sometimes outright fail my first time doing most things. I'm a natural at almost nothing. Eventually I get my bearings, find my legs, and can thrive where I'd once failed. Junior high was my first sign that I was not a sprinter but a long-distance man.

To be poor is to never quite warm up in the winter and never be truly cool in the summer. It is to use the stove for heat, and to work your wrist to soreness trying to create a breeze with a paper fan. It's wanting to stick your head inside the open oven like a freshly basted turkey, and to lay your head against the spinning wheel of your metal fan in search of relief from the humidity.

When you're poor you are always subject to the extremes of weather, 'cause your apartment is never really heated properly. You spend long winters with a slight chill in your bones that only hours in school can thaw out. When you're poor in summer you sit outside, find some shade, and luxuriate in any stray breeze that comes briefly, sweetly, your way. It is socks and sweaters to bed. It is sweat as second skin. It is figuring out that weather is a tool of an amused god used to illustrate just how brittle the walls of your apartment are and how little comfort your place of shelter really affords.

When we lived in the projects I remember how vulnerable my family was to the fluctuations of nature, and how flimsy was our grasp on security. My mother held my sister and me just above the poverty line for years—working poor but not homeless—before we actually started creeping up toward the middle class. But we never did live anywhere with serious central heating. So winter mornings—when the wind whips and my clothes seem to disappear in the face of arctic blasts—I always get pulled back to the days when I stood in front of the kitchen oven with outstretched hands, briefly warm when I was dying to be toasty.

Hot summer days remind me of roaches. Being poor in Brooklyn also meant having unwelcome little brown visitors. We never had rats. I saw a mouse now and then. But in a New York City housing project in the sixties and seventies roaches were to our life as blue sky was to someone in Montana. Live in a sixteen-story building packed with poor people, and maintained by a crumbling city's bureaucracy, and you'll have roaches, despite your mother's best efforts. To paraphrase a football cliché: You couldn't stop the roaches; you could only hope to contain them.

For years I used to worry that I'd be at school and a little brown roach would crawl out of a book, a bag, or even my shirt. No matter how you dressed or how poised you sounded, a roach's appearance just howled poverty like a wolf does at the moon. In the days before we finally moved out of the Tilden projects my mother was carefully looking through our clothes and belongings for roach eggs, determined to leave the projects behind and not bring any souvenirs with us.

Ma was, not surprisingly, considered uppity by a lot of our neighbors in the projects. She didn't sit outside on the benches and gossip. She didn't drink beer, play cards, and watch the "stories" (soap operas) with them. She wanted to move out of the projects. Who did she think she was? That's not to say my mother didn't have friends in 315 Livonia, but once she began attending night school in pursuit of her teaching degree, she poured all her heart into it. And that dream wasn't just to teach, it was to escape the vertical ghetto of the Tilden projects.

During our years there all the more ambitious and able residents of Tilden began moving out, relocating either to Queens, Long Island, or even back down South. When word got around that we were trying to move there was definitely lots of "playa hating." It was as if Ma's ambition somehow made others look bad. Even close friends and relatives doubted her. I'd overhear them on the phone questioning her, and Ma answering, "No, it'll be all right," "Yes, I can handle it," and "No, I can afford it." My sister, who as an adolescent grew more connected to the streets of Brownsville while I was withdrawing, was actually reluctant to leave the 'hood.

Ma was too stubborn to listen to the doubters. So one morning when I was fifteen, I left the Tilden projects for school in East

Flatbush and never came back. I took my usual route, one bus up Rockaway Boulevard and another out to East Flatbush, and then onto another bus or take the short walk to school.

But after classes I didn't head back to Brownsville, but went in the opposite direction, getting on a bus filled with more white kids than black. We headed in the opposite direction, going toward Mill Basin, a white enclave that housed South Shore, the biggest and newest high school in Brooklyn. In fact, I changed buses at Flatlands Avenue right across from South Shore, which gave me some trepidation, since they'd quickly emerged as Tilden High's fiercest athletic rival. Hoping the "T" stitched onto the back of my jean jacket wouldn't cause me any trouble, I got on the bus heading east in Flatlands. It took me through Canarsie and toward an unimpressive piece of real estate called Spring Creek.

My new bus ride on Flatlands actually ran parallel to my old journey toward Brownsville, but several important miles farther south. There were other black faces on this bus, but mostly my ride mates were Jewish and Italian. I felt very self-conscious, and there were definitely some hostile eyes on me. I'd traveled on the Flatlands bus before, yet always as a tourist, an outsider. Now this was my ride home, and I felt uncertain about claiming it.

Fights between white and black teens were regular occurrences in the contested streets of Flatlands, Mill Basin, and Canarsie. Kids from the rival schools, Tilden, South Shore, Canarsie, and Jefferson, battled at basketball and football games. I recall going to a football game during which the mostly black and Puerto Rican cheerleaders of Jeff bum-rushed the field while the mostly white Canarsie girls were still doing their routine, pushing them off the grass and onto the sidelines. Just as those tough Jefferson girls made it clear they were gonna take over the field to do their thing, blacks from the South and the Caribbean were steadily encroaching on white areas. My presence on this bus was just one more example.

While that racial turmoil concerned me, I was still overjoyed to be out of the Tilden projects. No more were we mice in the maze of a sixteen-story building. Now we were residents of a three-bedroom apartment in a two-story building we shared with three other families. These "garden apartments" filled one block of the Fairfield Towers. The other buildings were well-maintained apartment buildings with balconies. There were other apartment complexes in the area, as well as some blocks of two-family houses. A block away from our new home was a strip mall, and next to it an enclosed mall anchored by an supermarket.

In reality we were only two neighborhoods away from Brownsville, but the vibe in Spring Creek, at least when we first moved in, was more suburban than Brooklyn. In fact, right across Flatlands from our place at 1081 New Jersey Avenue was a huge tract of undeveloped land, which, one day, became the vast Starrett City development. But in the midseventies its only distinction was that Pennsylvania Avenue, the road that connected the area to the Belt Parkway, ran right through it.

I got off the bus at the intersection of Pennsylvania and Flatlands, walking through the supermarket parking lot to 1081 New Jersey, where, finally, I had my own bedroom. There I had my first desk, my own stereo system, and a closet where my comic book collection was replaced by copies of *Players* magazine, the black *Playboy*, which was brand-new then. I was fifteen, just starting high school, and it was the first time I'd ever had privacy in my life.

At last I could play BLS or eight-track tapes late at night, beginning my own personal education in pop music. I became obsessed with Sly and the Family Stone's *There's a Riot Goin' On*, playing "Family Affair" over and over at night, seeing in that lyric about estranged brothers a correlation with my increasingly contentious relationship with my sister.

Moving out of Brownsville didn't change things for Andrea, though, because, mentally, she never really left. While Ma and I were happy to have made the move, my sister missed the projects and would go back as often as she could. Ma and I were trying to escape the physical and mental limitations of life in the projects, whereas Andrea found a sense of community and personal freedom in that chaos.

Her deepest friendships remained the kids from the Tilden projects and schoolmates who resided in the Ville, while I bonded quickly with the more middle-class white and black boys and girls of Fairfield Towers. Years later I'd coin the phrase "ghettocentricity" in reviewing a rap album in the *Village Voice*. People thought my idea of a point of view so consumed with street values that everything else felt foreign came from listening to the music. In truth, ghettocentrity, like a lot of my ideas about the attraction of street life and urban culture, came from life in Brownsville and, in particular, my sister.

Even in this more middle-class development Andrea fell in with a local crew of tough girls who, not too long after we moved out there, turned against her. Sometimes they'd hang out under our window and call out threats to her. Andrea brushed it off. To Ma and me it was a strange twist. Here we were trying to avoid ghetto-style drama, and not a month or so into our new life, Andrea got into a beef with the only female roughnecks for blocks.

Andrea still carried the 'hood with her wherever she went, but for me, Spring Creek was a vastly different experience from Brownsville. When I played touch football and half-court basketball out with the Fairfield Towers crew, I balled with Italian, Jewish, and Irish kids, along with the blacks and Puerto Ricans. Even the brothers there were different from my Brownsville friends.

Whereas my old friend Dan Parks's Hendrix adoration was an anomaly in the Ville, out in Spring Creek I met black kids who blasted Gentle Giant, Genesis, and Jethro Tull. A couple of dudes I befriended were products of mixed marriages. They were teenage boys figuring out how to define themselves as men. Quite a few of them chose a "white" lifestyle, which meant rock music, dingy bell-bottom jeans, and no dancing at parties.

Hanging with them, I started listening to rock radio like WNEW-FM and WPLJ, New York's album-oriented rock powerhouses. I bought a Rolling Stones greatest-hits package, *Hot Rocks*, as well as the Beatles' catalog and lots of Elton John. I watched the movie version of the Who's *Tommy* a couple of times, and finally understood the difference between Pete Townshend and Keith Moon. I was proud to be the first person in my Spring Creek development to own Bruce Springsteen's *Born to Run*. I opened myself up to a side of pop music that I'd have been reluctant to publicly embrace in the projects.

I didn't get Led Zeppelin at first. It was loud and abrasive, with some vague mystical mess going on lyrically. Then Roland, a big, strong, half-black, half-German neighbor with a passion for football and marijuana, invited me to go visit a friend of his. Kevin was a frizzy-haired stoner whose bedroom was lined with black-light posters of couples performing the Kama sutra. There were two white parakeets in birdcages by his bed, and he had quad speakers sitting in the room's four corners.

I was never much into drugs. What had happened to my mother's friend Eddie had dulled my curiosity. Even when my friends started getting high in the 315 staircase, I usually passed. But Kevin had a bong, which I'd heard of but never seen, and he had hashish, which I knew of but had never smoked.

So Kevin lit the bong. He released the parakeets. He turned on a black light. I took a hit of hash. He put on Led Zeppelin's *Kashmir*. It flowed through the quad speakers. John Paul Jones's keyboards sounded majestic. John Bonham's drum kit boomed. Jimmy Page played resounding power chords. The birds flew over my head. The sexy couples seemed to be moving. I took another hit. I laid my head back. And in the moment of sound, vision, and drugs, finally, I understood Led Zeppelin.

After we moved out to Spring Creek I became a long-distance runner. Across the street from Fairfield Towers, where Starrett City now stands, were large tracts of empty land that on their far side abutted the Belt Parkway. On afternoons after school and on weekends, I'd run down Flatlands Avenue, past Fairfield Towers and private homes, and onto the dirt and scattered streets of asphalt on the edge of Brooklyn. Listening to my feet bounce off the ground and my own steady breathing (there were no Walkmen or iPods back then), I sought that so intoxicating runner's high. I loved the splendid isolation of running, and it spurred on my writing, driving me deeper inside my head, feeding a desire for introspection that was becoming a defining part of my personality.

I had dreams of running marathons and joining the Kenyans in the elite of long-distance running, but that idea died as soon as I joined the Tilden High School track team. Running solo had always been fun and relaxing. However, being timed and having to practice, and to have strategy meetings before competitions, sucked the spontaneity out of it for me. Plus, I wasn't that fast. Nothing like running through Prospect Park with several hundred other kids passing you by to clarify your place in the world.

I wanted to run at my own pace, but alas, my own pace was too damn slow. During one race in Prospect Park I tripped going through a big meadow with the finish line some two hundred yards ahead of me. Instead of getting up, I lay on the grass, listening to the thump of teenaged feet all around me. I watched the passing parade of high school colors from ground level. It was a strangely beautiful moment of defeat that I remember as one of the highlights of my track and field career. I can still feel that moment—the crisp air, the smell of the grass, a bruise on my right knee from falling, and my labored breathing. I'm a lot more sanguine about that athletic misadventure now because I understand that this failure, and what I felt, smelled, and saw, was part of my journey toward becoming a writer.

When I read over my short stories and diary entries from those years, they are filled with attempts to capture moments like my track and field stumble. Maybe it was because of all the Hemingway I was reading, but I was lingering a lot over passing moments—catching a breeze on a hot summer day, overhearing Al Green on a mailman's transistor radio, watching cute classmate Diane Dixon's Afro shift slightly in the breeze when the window opened in Spanish class.

Running and, more profoundly, writing were so seductive to me because they served (and still serve) as a form of meditation. Just as running put me in an introspective state, the act of writing itself felt lovely, often sensual. I loved how time passed when I was writing, that an hour, or two or three, would just disappear as I wrote on a notepad or banged at my mother's electric typewriter.

I'd already disconnected from organized religion, finding a very mercenary professionalism in most temples of worship that turned me off to most religions, including the Baptist denomination my mother was raised in. However, it was through these meditative moments that I had become aware that there was a heightened level of existence I very much wanted access to.

Lucky for me, it was writing that seemed to connect me to a higher power. I could also feel this connection when running, listening to music, and sometimes walking down the street (later I would add making love, but that wasn't happening in my teen years). But I could only consistently conjure it up when I put pen to paper. If my prose wasn't divine, and it rarely was, or is even now, the process of writing itself always was and is. As a result, the act of writing filled a spiritual gap in my life and fueled a work ethic that I, in retrospect, realize was a joy ethic. The more I wrote, the more likely I was able to invoke the deity inside me. So I became a most grateful workaholic, dedicated to writing something every day, no matter how small or inconsequential, as if I was praying to a God with no name.

TILDEN TOPICS

After reading all those great American novels I acquired through the Literary Guild, I'd imagined my future lay in writing a great American novel too. But in high school my focus slowly changed. I was writing tons of fiction and fictionalized stories. They filled up a green metal file cabinet—some typed, some handwritten, others just scrawls on bits of paper. At the same time, all of this introspection alienated me from people. As teenagers often do, I felt I wasn't connecting with my people, like I was standing outside of things, a state of mind that would intensify over time.

To combat that feeling I joined the *Tilden Topics*, the school newspaper, figuring that being part of it would allow me to ask questions, and asking questions would allow me to learn things about people, and hopefully about myself. Joining the *Topics* gave me an excuse to be nosy, and I exploited it, using my reporter title to fill my notebook with stories that were never written and quotes I never used. My output might have been limited, but these efforts pulled me out of my literary cocoon and into the world. For years afterward I used questions as conversation starters, and really tried to listen to people when they spoke to me, developing a patience for other people's musings that continues to serve me well.

It didn't hurt that Tilden High was at a turning point in its own history. The class of 1975 I entered the school with in '72 was predominantly white, but every class afterward was predominantly black and Hispanic, with a huge increase in West Indians. The white flight and black influx that I'd seen firsthand in Brownsville was occurring in East Flatbush. The civil rights–era tactic of school integration, alongside the failing city services of the seventies, was changing the color of my schoolmates with every semester. At local diners Jewish knishes were replaced by West Indian beef patties. In the surrounding streets the local accents were no longer Hebrew or Sicilian but patois. Soccer balls kicked by brothers in tams filled the air outside Tilden's gray stone front steps. Of course, the black/white racial tensions of the time flared up from time to time, but there was this new element in the mix—African American versus Caribbean American, niggers versus coconuts, soccer versus basketball. We resented their presence, and didn't understand their words, their food, or their attitude. All of which gave me a lot to write about, even if not a word of it would ever be published.

For the first semester of my senior year I participated in a citywide program that allowed students to work at a business four days a week, getting real-world experience in exchange for school credit. So from September to December 1974 I took the subway to Nevins Street, and then walked a few blocks over to Atlantic Avenue to the storefront offices of the *Brooklyn Phoenix,* a weekly that covered the brownstone areas of Boerum Hill, Cobble Hill, Park Slope, Brooklyn Heights, and Fort Greene (which I'd move into a couple of lives later).

The *Phoenix* was trying to carve out a niche as the chronicler of these "emerging" neighborhoods way before the banking establishment of the city decided to help with mortgages and loans. While the far end of Brooklyn, where I was living and going to school, was losing old-school white ethnics, the brownstone areas closer to Manhattan were just beginning to see signs of what we now call gentrification. The weekly's staff was filled with young, long-haired, white, liberal types, who had a rather condescending view of the blacks and Puerto Ricans these protoyuppies were replacing. I'm not sure if it was a little joke on their part or just insensitivity, but they gave me—the black kid—a regular assignment of calling the local precincts to write a police blotter column on local crime. I'd talk to the cops and write up muggings, breaking and enterings, and rapes. It was my first introduction to cop coinage like "perps" and their laconic attitude toward violence.

The schizophrenic nature of the journalistic lifestyle I observed almost put me off the profession. Every week the temperatures at the *Phoenix* rose as deadlines approached. People sniped at each other over editorial decisions, and erupted over edits. I watched with concern as these adults sparred. Once the paper was put to bed, the voices softened and wineglasses emerged, and everyone gathered together and went out to dinner. I'd never before seen the crazy mood swings endemic to this high-stress profession. If that was my future, I wasn't sure I wanted it.

Still, the idea that journalism could be more than just the facts, that it could even be an art form of its own, got into me. In the midseventies the phrase "new journalism" kept turning up in all the magazines I read, along with the names of its key practitioners: Tom Wolfe, Gay Talese, Jimmy Breslin, Hunter S. Thompson, Joan Didion, Norman Mailer. I reread James Baldwin's *The Fire Next Time*, now with a new appreciation for it as journalism, feeling a connection to it I'd never had to Baldwin's novels.

After my tenure at the *Phoenix* I began grabbing the *Village Voice* whenever I could. It was a weekly repository of new journalism, which is what first drew me to it. Quickly, however, I found that it was the *Voice*'s critics, particularly the lead film reviewer, Andrew Sarris, and his rock counterpart, Robert Christgau (who did a monthly "Consumer Guide" column on new albums and singles), that had me a regular reader. Through their erudite commentaries I learned about film genres and musical movements, and got introduced to Sarris's auteur theory and Christgau's prickly pronouncements.

Through their writings and the work of the many critics they edited, I found new names to study—James Agee, Georgia Brown, Ralph J. Gleason, Dave Marsh, and many others. I'd haunt the Brooklyn Public Library at Grand Army Plaza, each writer leading me to others, each cinematic or musical reference guiding me to others. Back at Tilden for my last semester, I felt suffocated taking classes and writing notes. I'd gotten a taste of a world out there that I was anxious to get back into.

In the meantime I continued to read and learn. Two books of criticism entered my consciousness, altering my perspective, though they were very different from each other. Missing from my readings in new journalism and cultural criticism were black voices. *Rolling Stone*, *Esquire*, *New York* mag, the *Village Voice*, and other temples of quality writing had precious few African American writers. The work of the few who cracked these markets seemed a touch soulless, as if they'd left the race card out of their deck.

Then I came upon LeRoi Jones's *Blues People*, his 1963 meditation on race, jazz, and the blues. It was the first serious work I'd read about the nexus of black music and American culture by someone who had grown up steeped in it, and it reverberated with me. Through Jones I was given a context to understand John Coltrane as a musician and spiritual figure, as well as the aesthetic gulf between the R&B world I'd been raised in and the rebellious free jazz that inspired Jones. Later I would quibble with elements of his argument, but the idea that our music was in a constant struggle with the forces of capitalism to define its own direction struck me as right on (and still does).

While by the midseventies *Blues People* was a widely acknowledged classic, Greil Marcus's *Mystery Train* was published in 1975 and, for me, remains *the* essential book of rock criticism. Marcus's goal was to help us see rock music as an extension of, and even an addition to, United States history, one that shed light on many of its unspoken mysteries.

Marcus, like most white critics, loved himself some Elvis. My feelings about Elvis pretty much correspond with those of Chuck D, so the lengthy Elvis material didn't mean much to me. However, two chapters in the book turned my head: his exploration of the demonic lore surrounding Delta bluesman Robert Johnson, and a stunning portrait of Sly and the Family Stone. I hadn't heard of Johnson before, or the tall tale of him selling his soul to the devil at a Mississippi crossroads. When I finally heard "Hell Hound on My Trail" and "Love in Vain," Johnson's voice felt as ancient as a tomb, and so dark it was hard to hear any other music for weeks afterward.

Quite simply Marcus's chapter on Sly's rise and fall, his impact on white rock and black pop, and his many mysterious decisions was the single best essay I'd ever read about a black pop musician. It became the model I aspired to as a critic (and still do). It hit me that hard. I read the Sly chapter over and over on the IRT subway, wondering how many years it would take for me to pen something as thoughtful and nuanced about the music I loved.

In May 1975, just before my graduation, I did a farewell column for the *Tilden Topics*. Looking back on it now, it reads like a precursor to the work I'd do later. It definitely sets up where I was in the world back in May 1975.

> On May 13 a meeting of the graduating seniors was held in the auditorium. Problems concerning graduation were discussed by teachers and then by students with opinions to express. These ex-Tildenites to be decided by a show of hands on the difficult (really!) question of what robes to wear to graduation. It was blue and black, thank you.
>
> Three years ago graduation seemed a lifetime away. 1975?! Hell, I'll be dead by then. But the time passed and after a couple of apparently dead summers and three seemingly boring winters, it's all over. During that period, many things ended; Richard Nixon's political career died of self-inflicted wounds, Reed and Dave DeBusschere retired, the Baltimore Colts collapsed, the energy shortage came and went (was it really here?), the Black Panthers disintegrated and everybody got bored with the space program.
>
> In that same span many things began: the Islanders were born, Abe Beame became mayor, the Boston Celtics were reborn, Jerry Ford went from frog to prince (remaining a frog at heart), the Miami Dolphins emerged as the Green Bay Packers

of the '70s, girls continued discarding outer garments to the fascination of the opposite sex (meaning me), the Vietnam War really ended and the painful reflection began. Muhammad Ali was champ again, while Elton John, Jack Nicholson, Bruce Lee, and Senator Sam Ervin all became superstars. The supermarket, the belly of America, was increasingly a very, very expensive place to visit.

A lot stayed the same, like the solid boring *New York Times*, the rising interest in nostalgia, the New York Rangers and the Dallas Cowboys in roles as perennial bridesmaids, Stevie Wonder stayed Stevie Wonder, Walt Frazier remained "Clyde" and Al Green stuck to his sound and no one argued with the results.

On the local front we lived through a passable production of *Guys and Dolls*, an almost great football team and then two lousy ones, two bad baseball teams and one almost good, three almost good basketball teams, a couple of small fires, more than one burglary, Mr. Morris and Mr. Goodman, a dead student union, an influx of West Indians and an outflux of white students. This, among other things, made up our collective history.

Doesn't seem right, does it? History is something written about people dead and gone, but we're still alive and going.

But, you'll see, things never really become old; they remain in our minds, as exciting, depressing, frustrating or funny as they were when you first felt it. Tilden High will always be inside you no matter how hard you try to forget. These three years haven't really ended and, perhaps, they never will.

NYC LATE SEVENTIES

It was a Wednesday morning in the late 1970s. I pushed myself out of bed, hearing the sounds of Miles and Monk in my head. As I looked out of my window at the presunrise darkness and the forlorn winter trees, I conjured "So What" and *Straight, No Chaser* in my ears to motivate me on an unforgiving day. I'd signed onto a history of jazz class that, due to its prime place in the curriculum of the fine Catholic university I attended, was scheduled once a week at 8:00 A.M. Determined to one day be the world's greatest music critic, I'd signed up enthusiastically, and then battled my common sense all semester to get to class on time.

Other than attending the St. John's jazz class this day would be typical of most others from the years 1977 to 1979, the years I traveled daily from East New York, Brooklyn, to Jamaica Estates, Queens, to Harlem, USA, to the heart of Times Square, and sites beyond. These were years when I spent a third of my day on an MTA bus or train, pursuing my dreams via the number 54 bus, the J train, the number 32 bus, the number 44 bus, the E and F trains, the D train, and the number 2 train home. I did homework on the buses. I wrote articles on the subway. I learned. I hustled. I made mistakes. I made friends. These were the years I studied the ways of magazines and record labels, gained role models and access to free tickets. I was an apprentice, and New York City was my mentor.

I'd won a scholarship to attend Oberlin College in central Ohio, via a competition presided over by legendary congresswoman Shirley Chisholm. A much smaller scholarship was available to me more locally at St. John's. My guidance counselor couldn't believe I wouldn't take the Oberlin offer and get the hell out of New York. But I wasn't gonna leave my mother and sister alone in Brooklyn. Moreover, I wasn't going to a school where the closest big city was Cleveland! Staying in New York to attend St. John's was absolutely the best decision of my life. New York may have been on the ropes financially, and in disrepute nationally, but it gave me an education impossible anywhere else in the world.

On this particular morning I wobbled out of my mother's home on New Jersey Avenue and walked a block over to Pennsylvania Avenue, where, along with a batch of schoolkids and workers, I shivered as we waited for the number 54 bus to take us up Pennsylvania Avenue, the major north-south artery of East New York. At Livonia Avenue the bus went under the elevated IRT line, the same train that for years ran past my window at 315.

A couple of blocks up from the elevated train we rolled by Thomas Jefferson High School, which in the seventies was one of the roughest, toughest schools in New York, and known for NBA-quality ballplayers (Sidney Green would rise from Jeff to the Nevada–Las Vegas Runnin' Rebels, to the Knicks) and for terrorizing kids from other schools. Even when I was in college I kept my eye on Jefferson students, female as well as male, because their fearsome rep preceded them.

Up past Liberty Avenue's A train stop, across Atlantic Avenue (and the bank that held my student loan), we navigated over to the J train, which held the distinction for being the slowest, most rickety subway line in the city. Back then most of the J stops in Brooklyn and Queens were elevated and without walls, so each time the doors opened a bitter gust of wind came through the train, blowing in tree leaves, rain, and sometimes snow. The cars were throwbacks, with no air-conditioning in the summer, except for small feeble fans, seats made of cushions that looked like kernels of corn, and all painted a drab industrial green. The whole experience was like being stuck in a Walker Evans New York City subway photo circa 1940.

As we rumbled through the unfashionable 'hoods of East New York and Cypress Hills toward Jamaica, I'd find a seat as far from the doors as possible and pull out a notepad. Starting in high school I became an inveterate scribbler, but it intensified in my college years. I had a little spiral notebook, so I could replace pages once the book was filled with my precious thoughts. I'd scribble in anything, though—black-and-white elementary school composition books, blank artist sketch pads, the backs of novels and textbooks.

Aside from documenting my teenage angst, this obsession had a very practical effect. I became a habitual, rather than instinctual, writer. That's not to say I've never been visited by a muse or got feverish with an idea. It happens all the time. But I don't need those things to happen. I write because I do. Rarely does a day go by that I don't put pen to paper, even if it's just to ask myself how I'm feeling. All the great musicians I've interviewed talk about woodshedding, playing for hours at a time, refining their chops. The same holds true for the workout regimen of great athletes. Gotta train those muscles. On the long rides to and from Queens, I trained daily with pen and paper.

Once the train arrived at 168th Street in Jamaica, I went downstairs and joined the mass of commuters at the bus depot. If Jamaica was the soul of black Queens in the seventies, then the bus depot was the heartbeat, where you boarded buses that connected Hempstead and Roosevelt with Cambria Heights and the white areas of Jamaica Estates, Corona, and Queens Village. There were white folks at the depot, but, by the late seventies, it was very much a black scene dominated by teenagers, who, despite the early hour, were already flirting and fussing in hormonal rampage.

The front and the middle of the bus toward St. John's would be jammed with adults, while kids ruled the back. Once past the bus's rear entrance you were in the smoking zone, with puffed Kools, Parliaments, and whatever other menthol brands they had gotten their hands on. The boldest among them started the day with a bit of reefer. One morning I saw a particularly progressive group with an expanding roach clip, so the holder could pass the joint down the line while never relinquishing control.

After people squeezed in from the E and F on busy Hillside, the bus rolled through Jamaica Estates, an area of large, leafy homes that folks in the smaller homes in Jamaica aspired to. After fifteen minutes St. John's appeared on the left side of the bus, up on high ground and ringed by huge parking lots that supported its commuting student body. While the lots were fine for automobiles, those wide open spaces created a vicious wind tunnel that made walking on campus in the winter a chilly nightmare.

After braving the cold, you reached a cluster of buildings, some Gothic, some nondescript and modern, that constituted the university campus. Thankfully, on this bitter morning, my jazz class was in the first building on campus, so that the shelter of its walls made up for its gloomy gray exterior. The jazz class was in the basement and taught by a bookish adjunct, a rather straight-looking dude who wore white shirts and a dark tie most mornings, like Miles's old pianist, Bill Evans.

Still, he was around thirty, which made him a youngster on St. John's teaching staff, and that he knew anything about jazz made him inherently hip at a very conservative place. I was already into Coltrane and Miles, but on those cold mornings I woke up to the energy of Louis Armstrong's Hot Five, the big band power of Ellington and Basie, the artfully enunciated sounds of Ella and Sarah Vaughan, and the eloquent syncopations of Monk.

This weekly immersion in jazz, augmented by compilations and best-of collections, filled in the blanks, not just in the journey of this special branch of music, but in the history of African American culture. The through line that struck me back in college, and would later inform my work, was the interconnected nature of black music.

So many of the famous players in jazz played R&B or blues and did session work for labels like Motown and Atlantic Records to feed their families. I didn't see the rigid distinctions between the genres of black music that the histories written about jazz, blues, R&B, gospel, and rock and roll in their narrow-mindedness suggested. Even back in college I could tell that these barriers were more the projections of the writers and members of the audience than of the musicians themselves.

From my reading and listening I was always struck by how many different things were happening simultaneously in black culture.

Since black people were so segregated for most of the twentieth century, and black radio so eclectic in its programming up until the seventies, I just felt that everybody in the community had an inkling of what was going on. Ray Charles may have been the rare musician with the freedom to explore the interconnections on record, but I was sure he wasn't alone in hearing them.

For years after that class I held on to my notes, partly because it gave me a very clear if simplistic historical outline of jazz, and also because I found it incredibly difficult to toss out anything related to black history. I was becoming a pack rat of books, newspaper clippings, magazines, and ticket stubs. It was the beginning of a just-in-case mentality that would make clutter a huge part of my living conditions.

For the rest of my morning at St. John's I'd work my way across the windswept campus, taking largely unmemorable classes in my major, communications arts.

As important to me as the jazz class in my development was a weekly class on foreign film by Professor Alan Seager. I'd read references to Fellini, Bergman, Kurosawa, Rossellini, and the other international masters in Andrew Sarris's erudite *Village Voice* reviews, but it wasn't until this class that I'd see any of their films. Over the course of one semester I saw *8½*, *The Seventh Seal*, *Yojimbo*, *The Bicycle Thief*, and a few other gems. Watching these varied and masterful films felt like an electric wire had been attached to my eyeballs.

Just as the records on my mother's hi-fi had given me some sense of America outside New York, these great foreign films showed me that America didn't have a lock on rich culture or cinematic art. It was years before I'd travel outside the States, but the work I saw in this class opened me up to the world. (Years later, when I became a director, it would be the work of foreign filmmakers that influenced me the most.)

Akira Kurosawa made a particularly strong impression, since the echoes of *Yojimbo* in Clint Eastwood movies were so obvious, and appealed to the Forty-second Street devotee in me. Moreover, I was happy to see nonwhite people onscreen in such rich variety and nuance. Kurosawa made masterful work outside of Europe and America that in fact influenced the cinemas of both. I became a Kurosawa fanatic, marching down to the Bleecker Street Cinema or up to the Thalia on the West Side for double features of *Yojimbo* and *Sanjuro*, or to see *Throne of Blood* and *Rashomon*. My first viewing of the three-hour-plus *Seven Samurai* made my head spin, since it so profoundly pissed all over *The Magnificent Seven*, Hollywood's pale version of his epic.

Kurosawa's huge vision, his ability to both manipulate masses of warriors and create scenes of quiet intensity, exploded with possibilities that the work of the European masters did not. Kurosawa willed into being a cinema of strength and nuance with nary a white man in sight. I had had no idea how much I needed to see films like these until I had. It made films deeply grounded in the specifics of ethnic group or national culture seem essential.

During high school I'd discovered that there was more to Manhattan than Times Square, a realization driven by cinema. Through the *Village Voice*, I learned about clubs and cafés in Greenwich Village that, once I turned eighteen and entered college, I began to frequent. But more important were all the art movie theaters around town. Across from Bloomingdale's on the East Side were the Baronet and Coronet, and a little farther up, their neighbors, the more sophisticated Cinemas I and II. Later I began haunting the downtown revival houses—the Bleecker Street Cinema, Theater 80, the Waverly (soon home of *The Rocky Horror Picture Show*'s midnight screenings), and the Elgin (where *The Harder They Come* would become a staple). Up on Fifty-seventh Street was the Playboy Theater, which had a one-dollar movie policy on Saturday afternoons for second-run features.

At the same time that revival houses and the *Village Voice* were expanding my mind, opening me up to ways of life I'd never known in Brooklyn, my interactions at St. John's were showing me the limitations of being parochial. In the cafeteria at St. John's Marillac Hall I saw every day that, despite better laws, the advances of the civil rights movement, and the hopes of the preceding generations, on an everyday basis real social integration was a struggle. By the vending machines were six to eight tables known as "the black corner," from which disco anthems flowed from boom boxes, and where girls practiced the hustle, and the African American community gathered to gossip, play the card game "spades," and, even, have lunch. In the pre-hip-hop era, before black street culture had become intertwined with white youth rebellion, there was a huge cultural gap between the black students and our white classmates. There were no "wiggers" at St. John's at that time, at least that I remember. If we were gonna have meaningful social interactions with our white schoolmates, it was usually on their terms (meaning listening to Billy Joel, wearing dingy jeans, or smoking hash, not cheeba).

There have been entire books written on the topic of black self-segregation in white college lunchrooms, so I won't devote much time to "the black corner," other than to note that its location on the St. John's campus was determined as much by finance as by sociology. HEOP (Higher Education Opportunity Program), which gave stipends to much of the black student population, was located down a hallway from the black corner, so kids congregated there to await meetings with advisers. Whether you received money from HEOP or not (I didn't), these tables had evolved into a central meeting spot on a campus where the black presence was otherwise limited to the basketball court.

It was in the black corner that I fell in with a crew who shared my interest in music. Some knew a lot about jazz. Others had the funk down pat. My closest friend in the bunch, Jared McAlister, had very eclectic tastes, and we'd talk music for hours, while lamenting the prevalence of Dan Fogelberg and Dave Mason on WSJU, the campus radio station, before heading off to our after-school gigs. Jared had landed a copy boy position at the *Daily News*, where he'd then stay employed as a reporter and editor for over twenty years.

Back then we were just young guys with dreams. We'd ride a bus from Utopia Parkway to Union Turnpike, a journey that took us past the Kew Motor Inn, a widely advertised short-stay hotel whose copy promoted waterbeds, Jacuzzis, and weekend rates. Among St. John's students it had a legendary status as the place for teachers and students, upperclassmen and coeds to sneak off for rendezvous.

I only had one assignation there, and it wasn't very sexy. She was a fair-skinned dancer with light brown eyes, who didn't attend St. John's, but lived out in the bougie enclave of Cambria Heights. Don't remember how I met her, but apparently she already knew of the Kew Motor Inn's reputation, and was intrigued enough to accompany me there one Saturday after her dance class.

When we checked in the dancer was given a flimsy bracelet, as a gift at the front desk, one that was already falling apart by the time we reached the room. It was an apt bad omen for our rendezvous. The room contained a king-sized bed with rose-tinted floral sheets, a mirror mounted on the ceiling, and an unappetizing view out the window of Grand Central Parkway. It was a ridiculously unsexy room. We lay on the bed and looked up at each other in the overhead mirror, feeling amused, embarrassed, and not very aroused. Being a boy, I still wanted to get busy, but my dancer friend, her curiosity about the Kew Motor Inn now satisfied, brushed off my advances and was out the door within a half hour of our arrival. Out about $120, not a small sum to a horny college boy, I contemplated phoning some other girls ("Hey, I'm in a room at the Kew Motor Inn. It's da joint. You wanna stop by?"). Thankfully, I thought better of that tactic, and went home.

Passing the Kew Motor Inn, a negative landmark in my young sex life, was a signal that the Queens part of my day was ending. At the subway I got off the bus and got on the E train for the next leg of my journey. I rode to Fifty-third and Seventh Avenue, transferring downstairs to the D train for the ride to 125th Street, and Harlem. Once off the train I wasn't walking across the franchise restaurant, highly gentrified, increasingly clean-cut boulevard of the twenty-first century. This 125th street was still ruled by heroin kingpins, numbers runners, and street hustlers of every variety. In this

Harlem there was no Starbucks or Pathmark, no Magic Johnson Theaters. Yet you could buy damn near anything on the street, from carburetors to law school textbooks to the contents of a woman's makeup case. Peddlers walked up and down 125th Street hawking in every barbershop, bar, and restaurant.

Harlem faces always seemed harder than those of Brooklyn folk. I mean, I came from Brownsville, so I'd seen my share of steely stares. Harlemites, however, just appeared extra raw to me, like there was a lower level of poverty and pain you accessed just living above 110th Street. Harlem girls definitely intimidated me. Felt like they were as likely to rip you off as kiss you. So I didn't try to be too smooth when I was uptown, saving my feeble game for the cuties I met out in butter-soft Queens.

The *Amsterdam News* was located on St. Nicholas Avenue, between 125th and 126th streets, around the corner from the Apollo Theater and across the street from the Nation of Islam bean-pie shop, a busy check-cashing place, and the Star-Lite bar, where vets of the paper got their afternoon taste. Classified advertising was on the ground floor, where rows of middle-aged sistas answered phones and kept an eye on all the building's visitors. To the left of the front door was a steep four stories of staircase. In my youth I took the steps two at a time, going past the administrative offices on the second floor and the comptroller on the third, and bounding up to the fourth, where editorial was located.

There I entered a long room of antique typewriters, dusty piles of newspapers and files, and overhead lighting that gave off the harsh neon aura of a 1950s pool hall. In general the *Amsterdam News* offices felt like an opened time capsule. The most modern fixtures in the space were the rotary phones, and they looked like they'd been installed during the Kennedy administration. The reporting staff, to my young eyes, was as ancient as the furniture. All of the male staff reporters (which means *all* of the staff reporters) were either gray or bald, and they had the bearing of men who had sat hunched over their whole lives.

There was "Tex" Harris, a feisty little light-skinned man who wore a jaunty French beret that belied a nasty mouth. Tex was the paper's Inquiring Photographer, whose head shots of ordinary Harlemites ran on the editorial page. However, Tex took much more pride in the cheesecake shots of young beauties that he pinned over his desk. There was Simon Anknewe, a grouchy, taciturn, pipe-smoking Nigerian who looked askance at everyone and everything.

Even more cynical than Anknewe was Les Matthews, aka Mr. 1-2-5 Street, a column that melded blind items, press releases, and gossip that glimpsed into the heart of Harlem. Les wrote terse one- and two-sentence items, like "James Jones made his singing debut on 125th street, while his father Jesse was iced on 116th street." This ex-boxer wore thick horn-rimmed glasses, and had tiny eyes and huge burly shoulders. Matthews typed hard with his two index fingers, punching the keys so hard he had to use three pieces of copy paper between his bottom sheet and his carbon, lest he punch holes in the paper. Les's laugh was harsh and dry, more sardonic than merry. The banter among all of these black journalists was bitter and caustic; they expected both white racism and black incompetence to rear its head in nearly every juncture of human existence. In their eyes, the *Am News* staff was rarely disappointed.

Less hard edged and marginally more optimistic was arts and entertainment editor Mel Tapley, an oatmeal-colored gent with a wiry black comb-over slicked across his head and glasses that were perpetually perched there, when not hanging upon the tip of his nose. Tapley's desk was a jungle of press releases, brochures, mail, and copy. He was a gentle man who had the demeanor (and cartooning skills) of a true artist and who, to take care of his wife and daughter, had taken on a demanding, not very rewarding 9-to-5.

The only two women in editorial were a study in contrast. Marie was an attractive, smallish receptionist who by day had to type memos and answer phones. By night she was a music columnist for the paper, feted by publicists and ass-kissed by R&B crooners. My presence at the *Am News* and growing interest in music would be an irritation to her, so we were never very friendly. Much nicer to me was Evonne Smith, who was the managing editor when I joined the staff as an intern. On a day-to-day basis she gave me assignments and made me feel welcome.

However, this was not a courtesy extended to her by the male staff reporters who worked under her. The old dudes at the *Am News* constantly challenged her authority, as if having a female boss was an insult. That Ms. Smith was a Muslim who wore her head wrapped may or may not have distressed the guys, but it certainly made her the target of off-color jokes, especially from the surly Tex.

The executive editor for much of my tenure at the *Am News* was James Hicks, who, in the civil rights era, had been a courageous, award-winning reporter. He'd been the one who allowed me to intern there, and, eventually, get paid for my work. But, aside from those two very good deeds, Hicks was an absentee manager who floated in and out of the office. Whatever fire he'd once had in his belly had clearly burned out by the late seventies.

The *Am News* was one of the many black institutions that had been energized by the civil rights movement, yet since then had struggled to find a mission. The place felt irredeemably trapped in the past. This malaise was bad for our readers and disappointing for the staff, yet fantastic for me. There were huge gaps in the *Am News*'s coverage, and I was able to exploit them. There was no one doing long-term reporting, so I was able to do a long take on the state of black studies at various city universities. There was sports coverage, especially of black college sports and street basketball, but little fresh reporting on major league baseball, the NBA, or the NFL.

Fortunately for me, I covered sports under the guidance of Art Rust Jr., a former NBC sports reporter and author of a trailblazing book on the Negro Leagues. Art had fallen on hard times professionally, and so worked part-time as sports editor at the *Am News*. Art unleashed me to go do profiles of everyone from Yankee pitcher Luis Tiant to New York Giants receiver Louis Gray. Though I enjoyed the opportunity to sit in the press box at Yankee Stadium, and to meet some legendary veteran sportswriters, I didn't actually enjoy the sports world. Too many locker rooms filled with surly, naked athletes. Too many jealous white reporters passing judgment on well-paid black men. In the reporters' greenroom at Yankee Stadium, where food and booze were free, I saw many famous bylines well lubricated by the third inning, and I found that disgusting.

What made the journeys to Yankee Stadium a bit easier was the presence of Willie Randolph. In a few short years my Tilden projects neighbor had made the leap from Brownsville's stickball games to the Pittsburgh Pirates, to manning second base at Yankee Stadium. When he joined the club via trade in 1976, Willie instantly solidified the infield and gave the Yankees top-of-the-lineup speed that made them pennant winners. Knowing there was someone I knew in that very intimidating locker room was comforting.

After all, this was the era of "the Bronx Zoo," where winning baseball and outsized ego were the norm at Yankee Stadium. But there were limits to our friendship. In the middle of one of those Reggie Jackson–Billy Martin blowups that marked the Bronx Zoo era of Yankee baseball, Art sent me up to the stadium to get Jackson's reaction to the booing, and to some racial epithets being yelled from the stands. When I told Willie what I wanted to ask Reggie, he begged off. Even though Willie wanted to help me, he knew messing with Reggie over something this sensitive was not a good way to keep in his hot-tempered teammate's good graces.

I understood. After all, I was the reporter. If there was a tough question to ask, I needed to do it myself. So I walked slowly over to Jackson's locker and, haltingly, introduced myself. The burly, bare-chested superstar studied me like an insect on glass. So I asked, "Do you think the fans' reaction to you is racially based?," trying to ask a potentially explosive question as inoffensively as possible.

Jackson stood up and yelled at me: "You're a black man, do I have to explain it to you?" Well, no, he didn't. He said something else equally harsh (but truthful), and then turned his back on me. End of interview. I took down his replies, and then got the hell out of there. With some massaging by Art Rust, this "interview" ended up as a front-page headline in the *Amsterdam News*. Something like "Jackson Blasts Racist Fans." Welcome to the world of journalism, kid.

The rough treatment I received from Jackson was just one of

many things that turned me away from sports journalism. For all my fan's awe of players' skills, and deep respect for reporters who wrote well on tight deadlines, there was an insular narrow-mindedness in the sports world that wore on me. Plus, I was more interested in what was happening in the South Bronx, a few blocks from the old ballpark. I covered the Yankees for the *Am News* during their back-to-back titles in 1977 and '78, the same years I was first discovering hip-hop in the city's parks and neighborhoods. What happened within the stadium's walls seemed a galaxy away from life outside on the BX streets.

While continuing to love sports, and to write about that world often over the years, I'd always be wary of how isolated it felt from the world beyond its boundaries. Ironically, the insular nature of movie reviewing and actor profiles, which could be as removed from the real world as George Steinbrenner's team, didn't turn me off. It didn't hurt that all media movie screenings and premieres were great free dates. The movie biz subsidized my love life during my college years, turning my skinny ass into a good date.

I was at a preview screening for *Star Wars* at the Loew's Astor Plaza, which had the audience rocking right from the opening crawl; *Close Encounters of the Third Kind* and *Apocalypse Now*, at the magnificent Ziegfeld Theater, which has the best sound system in the city; Woody Allen's *Annie Hall*, at Cinema I across from Bloomingdale's; *Saturday Night Fever* and *The Warriors*, in the Gulf & Western building screening room (now the Trump Tower). I was also at the legendarily horrific premiere of Michael Cimino's expensive bomb *Heaven's Gate* at Cinema I. One of my favorite films was *American Gigolo*, with its mix of materialism, sexual proficiency, and spiritual confusion that immediately spoke to me. I was awed to meet the director-writer Paul Schrader (who also penned *Taxi Driver*) at a press junket.

The best perk of my *Am News* years was a free trip to Las Vegas for a junket promoting the football flick *North Dallas Forty*. We out-of-town critics were put up at the M-G-M Grand Hotel and I, somehow, was awarded an amazing room with a burgundy platform bed with leopard trim and a huge overhead mirror. This monstrosity even had a goddamn gate around it. The bed was big enough for five couples to copulate separately and in peace.

So I spent my days in Vegas desperately trying to get women to come see my bed. Got a sista from Detroit to check it out, but only received a friendly peck on the cheek. I lucked out when I encountered a randy black woman broadcaster from Baltimore. The lady was about ten years older than me, but, I guess, couldn't pass up the chance to screw in that sick bed. I, in fact, became her Amtrak boy toy for several months, heading down to Maryland to lay up in her red waterbed.

The reason such a perk-filled gig was available was the unimportance of black film in the late seventies. The blaxploitation era had ended a good two years before I showed up at the *Am News*. While I was at the paper only a few black-themed Hollywood titles were released, with the lackluster *The Wiz* (starring Diana Ross, Michael Jackson, and Richard Pryor) and a few Pryor vehicles (*Which Way Is Up?*, *Greased Lightning*) constituting the feeble highlights.

On occasion a substantial work like *Brothers*, a fictionalized account of the relationship between the revolutionaries Angela Davis and George Jackson in the sixties, somehow sneaked through the system. Mostly I looked out for the odd juicy black part (Stan Shaw in the World War II drama *The Boys in Company C*) in an otherwise all-white flick. What ultimately made the film gig important in the long run, and as educational as anything I learned at St. John's, was my introduction to a community of emerging film archivists and independent filmmakers.

Just as I had with music, I made sure I read as many texts on black film as possible. Sadly, unlike jazz and R&B, the library was small: Donald Bogle's *Toms, Coons, Mulattoes, Mammies, and Bucks*, a survey history of the black image in motion pictures, was the gold standard, followed by Thomas Cripps's *Slow Fade to Black* and *Black Film as Genre*. There were a few collections of blaxploitation-era essays, and some photo books available, but that was basically it. The most provocative writings were those that depicted the work of pioneering filmmakers Spencer Williams and Oscar Micheaux, who made films in the prewar era expressly for Negro audiences.

Through the archival efforts of the scholar Pearl Bowser, you could catch screenings of Micheaux's work on occasion in New York. I recall seeing *Body and Soul*, Paul Robeson's feature film debut, at an unheated old Harlem landmark, the Renaissance Ballroom on 137th Street, and was amazed that there was this world that had existed outside the history books of American filmmaking. Working as a cinematic traveling salesman across the back roads of America, Micheaux had made a living with his films for decades, sustaining himself on guile and hustle.

The late-seventies equivalent came walking into the *Am News* office to meet me one day in 1978. Wearing a round Afro, a substantial beard, and a very serious demeanor, a young man named Warrington Hudlin introduced himself, his fledgling organization, the

Black Filmmakers Foundation, and the contemporary African American independent-film scene.

Where Micheaux was a carnival barker, making films that seethed with color and class conflicts, and the shame of illicit sex, Warrington introduced me to films that were earnest, political, and avowedly arty. Warrington's own meditation on working-class rituals, *Streetcorner Stories,* a cinema verité documentary, or Charles Burnett's neorealist drama *Killer of Sheep,* had nothing in common with Micheaux, blaxploitation, or anything Sidney Poitier had ever made.

This new black cinema, sadly, existed only in museums, film festivals, and on college campuses. Virtually none of the films I was seeing and writing about got a commercial release. At best they might be grouped in a festival with white-themed independent films (like the American Maverick series in the East Village), but even that was rare. (Burnett's *Killer of Sheep* didn't get a commercial release until 2006!) When I wrote about these works there was often griping at the *Am News,* since, unlike Hollywood dreck, these folks weren't gonna buy an ad unless it was purchased for a museum screening series. Better for me to use our film news hole to write up the James Brolin vehicle *The Car,* perhaps the worst movie ever made, rather than Roy Campanella Jr.'s short film *Pass/Fail.*

At this time even white indie film was still a relatively new idea, so the thought that there could be a black cinema outside Hollywood was not simply foreign to the cynics at the *Am News,* but downright ridiculous. My biggest challenge was not to accept the defeatism of the paper's staff. Meeting people like Warrington and the other black indie filmmakers was crucial in allowing me to see possibilities, and not limits, in the future.

After I'd turn in my stories and pick up assignments from Mel or Art, I'd walk down one flight to the comptroller's office to turn in my time card. Though I was technically an intern receiving college credits for my work, I'd also arranged to get paid for working at the *Am News*. It never came to more than $120, and sometimes was as low as $89 in any given week, but for a twenty-year-old college student in 1977 or '78, that was good money.

However, my treatment by the *Am News* comptroller was rarely respectful. They'd never pay me in time to cash the check at a bank, always after 3:00 P.M. So I'd have to go across the street to the nearest check-cashing place. A check-cashing place in Harlem circa late seventies was a spectacle, filled most afternoons with minimum-wage workers, public assistance folk, and everyone scrambling to make ends meet. There were always one or two dudes lingering around to see who left the cashiers' window with the fattest roll of bills.

After stuffing my money deep in my pants pocket, I'd walk across 125th street, past Bobby Robinson's long-running record store (he'd sign Kool Moe Dee's Treacherous Three and Grandmaster Flash and the Furious Five to Enjoy Records, the label he ran out of the back room) and the Charles's Gallery nightclub (where Russell Simmons saw Eddie Cheeba and first got turned on to rap music), before I went down into the BMT station for the A train downtown.

It was about 4:00 P.M. and time to switch gears. I'd been a St. John's student and *Am News* staffer. Now I was to adopt the third persona of my apprentice years—*Billboard* magazine stringer. On the A train down from 125th Street I'd look into my book bag to make sure I had any concert reviews or stories I had written for

Billboard, checking again for typos and misspellings. By the time I got off at Forty-second Street and Eighth Avenue, I was ready to navigate the streets of the not so great white way. There were peep shows up and down Eighth Avenue, including the huge Show World sex emporium between Forty-second and Forty-third streets. On Forty-third off Eighth was a beat-down diner I frequented along with hookers, cops, and *New York Times*men.

On Wednesday afternoon the streets were filled with folks exiting Broadway matinees, vendors legal and illegal hawking wares, and the hurly-burly of folks doing their everyday dance. This wasn't the post-Giuliani Disneyfied Times Square. In the Times Square of my memory there were not yet any Starbucks or megastores but plenty of pimps, break dancers, and three-card monte players. At 1515 Broadway, right around the corner from the Astor Plaza Theater, *Billboard*'s offices were up on the forty-third floor. In contrast to leaping up the long staircase at the *Am News*, I floated up in a modern Midtown elevator. I'd be buzzed into the office by the receptionist, then walk down a flight to *Billboard*'s editorial and advertising offices.

Sitting at a desk in the production area office was my great benefactor, Robert "Rocky" Ford Jr. I'd met Rocky in the fall of 1976, when I went with an old high school pal to see Graham Central Station headline a show at the Upper West Side's Beacon Theater. Sly's ex–bass player Larry Graham had organized a hot band of his own that had a funky instrumental out called "The Jam."

When we got up to the theater at Seventy-fourth Street and Broadway, we found that Graham's gig was part of a concert series called California Soul, aimed at branding Burbank-based Warner Bros. Records in the black music biz. Aside from Graham Central

Station, Al Jarreau, Ashford & Simpson, George Benson, and other recent signees were performing during this weeklong showcase. Warner Bros., like CBS and RCA, was intent on creating an identification with black music buyers that Motown, Stax, and Atlantic had organically.

However, the economic forces at work in black music weren't yet my concern. I was there to dance and look at girls. Which was what I was doing when Graham Central Station closed with "The Jam." I was sitting in the back of the orchestra and, like the entire crowd, I rose to dance in my seat. Well, everyone but one guy. Through the sea of gyrating bodies I spotted a man with a big Afro sitting down and writing in a reporter's notepad with a lighted pen. Whoa! A real rock critic in the flesh.

Once the show ended I pushed and shoved my way through the crowd, trying to find the brother in the Afro. On the sidewalk outside the Beacon I saw him, and, to be honest, he was an odd sight. He was extremely light skinned, with a big head adorned in metal-framed glasses, a bushy mustache, a light-colored jacket, jeans, and black-and-white saddle shoes, like someone in a *Happy Days* episode.

Despite his eccentric appearance, I approached him and his sexy, dark chocolate girlfriend and introduced myself. Robert "Rocky" Ford wrote reviews for *Billboard* magazine, though his nine-to-five job was working in *Billboard*'s production department. His date was a woman named Gail McLean, who was polite but clearly irritated at my intrusion. Rocky gave me his card and told me to send him some of my reviews.

Through a friend, Martin Baskin, I'd actually published a couple of record reviews in the Pace University newspaper (the editors never knew I wasn't a student). One was of the O'Jays' *Family Reunion* and the other of Paul Simon's *Still Crazy After All These Years,* both of which remain two of my all-time favorite records. I also sent him a few of my *Am News* clippings. Rocky liked my writings, and invited me up to *Billboard*'s Times Square offices, which had a spectacular view of Broadway and out to New Jersey, where they were building the new Giants stadium.

Just as heady as the view through *Billboard*'s big picture windows were the staggering amount of records casually lying around. At each writer's cubicle, and in glass-enclosed editors' offices, was enough vinyl to fill J&R Music World several times over. Almost every record released got a mention of some kind in *Billboard,* and the staff writers took their free goods for granted. As a vinyl-hungry college boy it was stunning to see all that music just lying underfoot. Those visits to *Billboard* were like trips to vinyl junkie heaven, and I never left without 45s, 12-inches, cassettes, or albums under my arm.

At first I was a mascot, just happy to be there. Eventually I got to know the editors and the staff, an eclectic group of music heads, serious journalists, part-time flacks, and full-time eccentrics who, along with Rocky, showed me the music-biz ropes. There was Adam White, the future editor-in-chief, a taciturn Brit with an encyclopedic knowledge of Motown soul; Roman Kozak, a balding punk rock connoisseur with a hard-on for the Plasmatics' Wendy O. Williams and a love for spicing his iced tea with alcohol under his desk; and Radcliffe Joe, a pipe-smoking, blazer-wearing West Indian cherub, who served as disco editor. Either by example or by giving me assignments, these gents granted me entry into the world of the record business and music criticism.

Through them I attended press parties and learned you could judge a good one if the buffet featured fantail shrimp and rare roast beef. I learned to refer to records as "product," and that free promotional records could be sold in bulk for cash to retailers. I learned that most music-business lifers were cynics and dreamers who knew that payoffs could make hits yet still believed in the transcendent power of music. From them I got my first taste of the backstage stories and secret history of American music that never ended up in the pages of *Billboard*, and rarely anywhere else.

My first *Billboard* piece was a profile of Evelyn "Champagne" King, a strong-voiced teenager from Philadelphia who had a disco smash with "Shame." That was followed by an interview with Bernard Edwards and Nile Rodgers, the bass and guitar duo behind Chic, who'd go on to have impressive careers as producer and writers. Radcliffe Joe gave me those first two gigs, which gave Roman the confidence to begin assigning me concert reviews. While Radcliffe had me covering the emerging disco scene, an area none of the vets at *Billboard* cared about, Roman sent me out to review music from the industry's other bastard genres—heavy metal and blues-based guitar rock.

So my black Brownsville self was soon found reviewing British blues-based rock bands like Foghat, Bad Company, Foreigner, and Hot Tuna (and silently thanking my Spring Creek friends for the ear-splitting education a few years back). There was one double bill I'll never forget—AC/DC opening for Ted Nugent at the Garden. Those two combined for a night of sonic sludge my eardrums have never forgotten. I took to buying packets of tissue paper to stuff in my ears whenever Roman sent me out. *Billboard* afforded me a real schizophrenic existence. One night I'd find myself at a gay disco in the West Twenties reviewing Sylvester. The next I'd be at MSG, surrounded by white kids in football jerseys shooting off firecrackers as Bad Company did an encore.

As I turned in my copy, I'd start harassing Roman or Radcliffe for my next assignment. Between the *Am News* movie screenings, the *Billboard* music reviews, and actually studying for St. John's tests, my nights were full during those hectic years. Once I had my assignments, I'd call around to line up some dates.

As my adventure in Vegas suggested, through my access to events I met older, more sexually active women. I didn't get any handsomer or dress any better (style never being one of my strong suits), but I became a more exciting date.

I'll never forget going to LeMoche, a big disco on Eleventh Avenue, to review the female disco trio First Choice, and spotting this big-bodied sister standing in front of me. She was tall, with wide hips and nice shoulders and sexy strong legs. Her hair was slicked back and tied into a small bun. When she turned to talk to her girlfriend, I saw her face—she was light brown with a wide mouth and sweetly protruding lips. I smiled. She smiled. Her name was Evelyn. She was Jamaican, lived in Flatbush, and had her own apartment. Most important: She thought I was cute.

At this point in my life I'd never actually spent the night at a woman's house, since none of my girlfriends had had their own places. Evelyn, god bless her, changed all that. I remember she had a tidy little Flatbush apartment in the era when West Indians were pushing out the Jews and Italians.

She had a small sofa, but what I really fondly remember is her silver beanbag, which was cool to watch TV in as well as being a sex enhancer. Evelyn and I discovered a variety of ways to get busy using that beanbag on our first night together. I remember how both confusing and liberating it felt to wake up in a strange bed, to smell her perfume in the sheets, to see the beauty products in her bathroom, and to shower using her soap. The fact that this was my first overnight visit with a woman wasn't lost on my family. When I stumbled home that next afternoon, as bleary-eyed and tired as I'd ever been, Andrea took one look at me, said, "It's about time," and then started laughing.

My maturation as a sexual being came at the tail end of the sexual revolution. Though the sixties is still associated with the "free love" period, the looser morals that were unleashed carried over well into the eighties. In the now distant pre-HIV era, condoms were optional. I carried condoms, but only used them if the woman insisted, and a great many women didn't. They'd use the curved plastic diaphragm, which I sometimes helpfully inserted for them. Or they used the IUD, a stringy, weird contraption that, if not put on properly, could pop your penis in the head. A few women, Evelyn included, utilized pills inserted in the vagina that would dissolve and generate a green sperm-killer foam. This stuff was a real joy killer, since the foam would sometimes slide into my tip and burn like hell. Moreover, once this stuff dissolved there was no oral sex for her, since it tasted like disinfectant.

Evelyn, as my first true mature lover, taught me much, and after a while she was suggesting that I move in with her. Evelyn was thirty, and I was about twenty-one, so I was in neither the financial nor psychological space to do as she wished. Our parting was bittersweet, since she wanted more than I knew I could give. I have to admit, this would not be the last time I'd part with a woman over my inability to give my heart.

After I'd used *Billboard*'s phones to make my personal calls, and listened to the gossip about Springsteen, or debated Steely Dan's latest effort, I'd go through the staff writers' pile of reject records, stuff as many as I could carry into a bag, and head out into Times Square toward the IRT subway home. I'd usually wait until after rush hour was over, and the commuters had thinned out, so I'd have room to pull out my notepad and start scribbling again. I had a long subway ride ahead of me from Midtown Manhattan, way out to Pennsylvania Avenue, the third-to-last stop on the New Lots Avenue line.

On my ride home, I was writing when a newspaper blew against my leg. I looked down, and, whoa, it was the *Am News*. Even more ironic was that this particular crumbled bit of newsprint contained three bylined stories by me; all my work on the subway floor, looking as disposable as a candy wrapper.

Unfortunately, this accident would come to foreshadow my immediate future. When I graduated from college in June 1979, my future looked good. I had income from two steady writing jobs (plus freelance assignments coming in) and access to all the cool free stuff I could handle. Plus, I was still living at home, so I could save money. I felt like my postcollege years were gonna be sweet. Then reality hit me hard, real hard.

THE WHITE LINES THAT BIND

The Pink Tea Cup is an anomaly, a soul food restaurant in the heart of the West Village that has survived for decades. When I first started eating there in the late seventies it was on Bleecker Street near Grove. I'd get an order of fish with greens and macaroni and cheese to go, and then carry the meal in a brown paper bag west toward the piers. These were the glory days of the gay liberation movement, so I kept my eyes to myself, not wanting to suggest to any of the friendly gentlemen who strolled its curvy streets that I wanted to hook up.

About a half block from the piers, where transvestites ruled and truck drivers snoozed, and blow jobs were the coin of the realm, I walked into a garage with my soul food feast. Sitting in the booth where drivers checked in before parking their cars was Nelson Elmer George. Throughout my college years and into my early twenties, I tried to bond with my father. My mother, who'd heard me whine and even cry about not having a father, reluctantly encouraged me, knowing it might help me become a man but worried I'd eventually be disappointed.

As I said earlier, my first really vivid recollection of my father is our weird trip to Harlem, where I got my first inkling of how, if not why, he got his hustle on. The irony was that I'd become something of a hustler myself, roaming the same nocturnal boulevards in search of money and fulfillment. The huge difference was that nothing I would do, or even seriously contemplate, would come close to crossing the line between the legal and illegal. To paraphrase Rakim, "I knew the ledge."

One of the things that came out of my visits was an article in the *Amsterdam News* called an interview with Mr. C., and it was billed as the reflections of a small-time drug dealer, which it was. The article was a way I could justify hanging with Nelson Elmer to myself—I was finally getting something tangible out of him. It was a way for him to explain his life to me, which he very much wanted to do.

Apparently my father's life changed in 1957, the year I was born. Unfortunately, the turning point in his life wasn't my birth, it was his first visit to a Harlem after-hours club on 122nd Street called Cary's. "It was in the basement of a building," he told me. "I came with a friend who was known there. They were very careful to see if you had any weapons before they let you in. There was a bar section, and people were sitting and drinking and smoking reefer, which seemed to be the main feature of going to this type of place. I was always a fella out in the street as well as being a working man. So I became acquainted with all the ways people made their livelihood. I met all the hustlers and all the hustles."

It sounded like dialogue from a Chester Himes novel, except for this man in a garage mechanic's uniform enjoying his macaroni and cheese, this wasn't a hard-boiled narrative but his life or, at least, his version of it. When I asked him about Pete Smith and he told me he was also known as Joe Robinson of the Bronx's Grand Concourse, or Clarence Robinson of Far Rockaway, Queens, I realized that his identity had been as fluid as his job status.

In the years since he and my mother separated, Nelson Elmer had been a merchant seaman, a doorman, a short-order cook, a onetime bar owner (apparently his partner, a woman, shot at him), and a low-level coke dealer. "I sold cocaine because it meant quick, easy money," he said. "I sold only cocaine. Exclusively. Never marijuana. Never anything else. Cocaine meant fast money. Nice clientele, clean clientele. Selling any other drug, you run into the scum of the earth, and I didn't want to be bothered. With cocaine, you only deal with kings and queens and heads of state. Just worked with blacks, too. Never sold a grain to a white man. Nothing. They were bad news to me, baby, especially when it comes to drugs.

"Because I usually had a regular job somewhere, I was never forced into dealing with heavy drugs. Cocaine was my gravy money. I'd spend a few hours every day selling it. But mostly I worked, so they came to me, and not the other way. People called me because I had good stuff. I sold in bulk, and didn't want to see twenty-five dollars or thirty dollars anytime. I bought my stuff wholesale, then sold it at up to 100 or 200 percent profit. I always sold it in large amounts, never small. In Harlem, my deals ranged from $250 to about $300."

We were speaking about the drug world before crack, a *Super Fly* world of cozy clubs where adults did their business in peace. That world was already disappearing in the early eighties, as angel dust, heroin, and aggressive young dealers were escalating the violence. In his mind Harlem had "got real mean." Nelson Elmer viewed this "heavy drug scene" with worry. Just as the music uptown was shifting from disco soul to beat-oriented rap, the drug scene was undergoing generational change too.

In relating his gangster tales my father provided me with a great unintentional "just say no" lesson. It started with his observations about "bag followers." These were "girls who like cocaine but have no money, so they hang with a dude until they sniff up his blow, and then move on to the next sucker." Then, without remorse, Nelson Elmer told his son, "I had two women in bed with me and some coke on [the] night table, and decided I'd rather have a blow than get blown."

Young and horny as hell, I figured any substance that could overwhelm a man's sex drive was to be avoided at all cost. On the heels of the tragedy of my mother's friend Eddie Sawyer, and my father's story, I have never allowed a line of coke near my nose. So I could never say that this man never did me any good.

Over time he'd show me more bits of his world. One evening he took me with him uptown. We hit the Big Track, a Harlem gaming joint where there was action twenty-four hours a day. We stopped at a bar near Esplanade Gardens where a thriving numbers operation was headquartered, and he went in the back to do a little business. We ended our little tour at a ragged tenement building just around the corner from the numbers bar.

Up two flights was an apartment with a red door. Nelson Elmer knocked. A dark face peered through the peephole. After being scrutinized, we were granted entry into a room awash in red. The lights, the carpet, and the bar were all red. Our host was named "J.C." He was a balding brown man in a chocolate-colored suit and a black turtleneck. He and my father were old running buddies from many Harlem nights, and I enjoyed watching Nelson Elmer's casual camaraderie, though it struck me that these dudes were closing in on the end of their good times, and he seemed to know it.

He said that he was gonna retire from his fun part-time gig. Number one, his connection had gotten busted, and he "could no longer get what I wanted. See, that's why having a job was so valuable. I didn't need to go to somebody else 'cause it wasn't my entire livelihood. When you're in the street, you always need backup of some kind. Besides . . ." He paused. "I have been feeling some vibrations. Nothing certain. Just enough to make me feel nervous, and when you get nervous in the street you definitely have to go. That is no place to be nervous."

On this foundation of lightweight gangster tales a détente grew between us. But the hustler in him couldn't be abated. At one point he wanted us to become a father and son process-serving team. His argument was that we could make quick cash and hang out together. Instinctively, I thought that that was a gig that could easily go bad. Serving the wrong man on the wrong day could be a very unpleasant business. Ma, as usual when it came to things related to Elmer, just laughed when I brought it up. She wasn't going to let that happen. This era of good feeling between my father and me would unfortunately be short-lived.

Perhaps it could have been the beginning of a strong father-son connection. After all, we shared DNA, looks, and an attraction for nightlife. For years I had thirsted for his company, feeling a primal need for a father and hoping, through him, to perhaps understand myself better. But I was in my twenties now. I had my goals to pursue and my own journey to take. Whether my father had been around when I was six or thirteen didn't matter now. What mattered were the decisions I made.

As a child, your parents define your world. As an adult, your decisions define your character. Between my mother, my peers, and the people I was encountering as a journalist, I was developing my own view of the world and, it hit me, I didn't need my father's. Over the next thirty years our contact would be brief and, mostly, superficial. It would no longer be his fault. It would be my choice.

NYC EARLY EIGHTIES

I graduated in June 1979 from St. John's University. The seventies had been a rugged time for my hometown. The Bronx was burning—literally. The city had basically gone bankrupt under the burden of unchecked municipal spending, institutional corruption, and an eroding tax base. Every night Johnny Carson made jokes about muggings in Central Park, helping poison the city's image around the country. Every great crime film of the era (*The Godfather, Serpico, Dog Day Afternoon, Shaft*) painted the place John Lindsay had labeled "Fun City" as a cesspool of unrest and suffering.

Yet, on those same streets, new dreams were being hatched and old ones fulfilled. My peers and I, about to enter adulthood under throwback president Ronald Reagan and aggressive mayor Ed Koch, were going to help reinvent New York by dreaming big and working harder than we'd ever thought we could. The transition from the seventies to the eighties can be defined by one word: ambition. It burned in us and lit up everyone I knew. This wasn't civil rights movement "we shall overcome" optimism, but a desire to take advantage of all the doors that that struggle had opened. Oliver Stone, who wrote *Scarface,* and then wrote and directed *Wall Street,* captured the aggression of the era, and of my reawakening city. Though I have never done cocaine, there's an anxious mania for movement that the drug instills that I felt all over New York. For good and bad, the city's 1970s financial despair was turning into a 1980s of greedy productivity. I never snorted the drug, but I did partake of the frenzy around me.

Looking back through my notebook pages from the era, I see I ached to do something, to be someone, to make my name mean more than it had when my father and grandfather were the only Nelson Georges in the world. I'd roll around my bed at night frustrated if I felt I hadn't worked hard enough, or anxious if I thought I hadn't worked well. I'd think there was a white writer out there who was already out ahead of me, who could afford to relax, and I'd jump out of bed and start writing. I don't think I was at rest the entire decade. The dawn of the eighties would inaugurate a new era in my life, and, happily, in the city I loved.

It was also when my troubles began. Within months of my graduation, my sister announced that she was pregnant, which meant I needed to move out so she could have my room for the baby. Then, one afternoon that summer, there was a letter waiting for me when I came to the *Am News*'s office. It said that due to budget cuts I was being laid off. Of course I was devastated. I tried to put a happy face on it. I'd started as an intern, so I suggested that I still write for the paper—after all, the perks were what really made it so valuable.

The management team that had allowed me into the *Amsterdam News* had been fired. The old-school reporters at the paper, who had Newspaper Guild protection, didn't stick up for me, nor were they particularly upset that I was out. So whether I was being paid or not being paid, I was no longer going to be allowed to write for the *Amsterdam News*.

At least I still had *Billboard*. After all, wasn't that the better gig? I went up to their offices one day later in that first postcollege summer, and was told that I was now banned from the publication. The LA-based editor-in-chief had sent a memo to New York stating that I used "black English" in concert reviews, and that I misspelled the name of Weather Report's Joe Zawinul in a review.

After my comfy college years, the real world hit me with three swift, hard, gut-busting blows. The only relief in this bad news was that Rocky Ford was getting an apartment in Jamaica, Queens, and was gracious enough to allow me to be his roommate. At least I wasn't starting my adult life living in my mother's basement, which I've always thought was for lazy losers, neither of which I had any intention of being.

I filed for, and got, unemployment via the *Am News*. It came to about forty or so bucks a week, beating a blank, though it did little for paying my half of the rent. So I lived the hustling life of a freelance writer, crafting press releases for publicists and writing four to five articles a week for as little as fifty dollars a shot. Rocky had hooked me up with a nice gig writing music news every month for *Musician* magazine, while I also ground out profiles for teen rags like *Black Beat*. Rocky was subsidizing my half of the rent with his *Billboard* money and a record-label advance for a 12-inch single by Harlem MC Kurtis Blow. Rocky, along with another *Billboard* friend, J. B. Moore, had decided to invest their money and time into making a novelty Christmas record with Blow, feeling that the rap scene in New York was a trend they could use to establish themselves as record producers.

But, while hip-hop's journey from street style to recordings was being hatched in our living room, I was struggling to make ends meet. It was a battle I'd wage from the summer of '79 right through all of 1980. During the many months when I questioned both my ability and my dreams, New York sustained me. By plugging into its places and spaces, I felt like the city was keeping me afloat. One asset was my relationship with Birdel's record store, a classic mom-and-pop store located in Brooklyn, at the corner of Nostrand and Fulton, near the A train.

Birdel's speakers were a daily announcement of the newest grooves in R&B and gospel. Inside was a narrow room with a low ceiling, covered top to bottom with racks of records, posters, top ten lists, flyers for concerts, autographed photos of singers, and a fine dusty mist created by the steady decomposition of the old albums in the racks and the foot traffic from the street. Birdel's high priest was Joe Long, a raspy-voiced man with black-framed glasses, a thick mustache, a modest Afro, and thick hands that either held 45s hooked around his index finger or rapidly racked up sales on the cash register. Ask him if Gladys Knight & the Pips had a new record, and his answer was always, "Right here!" and he'd turn around to where the latest 45s lay stacked like pancakes. If you said, "I don't know who made it, but it's about fishing in the sea," Joe would say "Marvelettes," and place the record on the miniturntable near the counter and "Too Many Fish in the Sea" played for you on a Saturday afternoon.

Joe dated a friend of my mother's, so I'd always looked forward to stopping, knowing there could be a free 45 in it for me. When I became a reporter, Joe became a source of info about the contentious, often poisonous, relationship between black mom-and-pop stores and the major companies that took over black music in the seventies and eighties. Those labels gave big retailers all the discounts, and, because they bought in bulk, better billing terms. Slowly, the combination of competition from bigger retailers, the conflicts with the major labels, and the decay of the business strips in the Bedford-Stuyvesant community ate away at Birdel's business, forcing Joe, and his peers nationally, to abandon competing in pop and R&B music and to begin emphasizing gospel, Caribbean, Latin, and other niche markets.

Early in their existence, rap records created one of those niche markets. I have a vivid memory of traveling out to Bed-Stuy in the fall of '79 to gauge the impact of "Rapper's Delight." When I arrived, the Sugarhill Gang was on the speakers outside, and the store was filled with a steady stream of people asking for the single. The 12-inches didn't even have the blue Sugar Hill Records label—just orange labels with Sugarhill Gang in black type. Joe was behind the counter, making change and selling this hot record like it was the glory days of Motown. My understanding of hip-hop's early appeal came from watching customers buy "Rapper's Delight" at Birdel's.

Just as influential in helping me keep my musical instincts sharp was J&R Music World on Park Row across from City Hall. Back before superstores and downloading, tasteful, full-service record stores kept the culture going, and J&R, located in a few cramped basements, was one of those places. I bought lots of jazz and blues at J&R. I'd read Charles Keil's *Urban Blues* or an article by Robert Palmer in the *New York Times* or Gary Giddins in the *Village Voice*, and I'd go to J&R to buy Bobby "Blue" Bland's *Two Steps from the Blues* or John Coltrane's *Giant Steps*.

My trips to J&R provided more than musical adventures. These Saturday trips to that record store introduced me to a discovery of lower Manhattan. After buying albums I'd walk past City Hall and across on Chambers Street to West Broadway where I took to eating souvlaki at Adelphia, a Greek diner. Thus fortified, I'd head uptown through the aging warehouse area that wasn't yet called Tribeca. It was just adjacent to City Hall, and neither fashionable nor cool.

More memorable was Soho, which was not yet an arty destination, more just a gateway to the West Village. It's impossible for anyone who wasn't in New York back then to understand now how dark and unpopulated the old industrial area between Canal and Houston was at the dawn of the eighties. I remember shafts of light cutting through the thick air on Mercer and Wooster, and the padlocked doors on innumerable gray, cast-iron factory buildings. I'd walk into art galleries on occasion, where I'd see carefully mounted rocks or odd shapes on wood floors. It was mystifying to me how these galleries survived.

Just as confounding were the sounds of music that would float down from open loft windows and catch my ear. Soho's empty industrial spaces attracted art dealers and jazz musicians. Unlike the mainstream players at the Village Vanguard and the Village Gate just a few blocks uptown, these loft jazzmen tended to be younger, lesser known, and more experimental. A spot I often visited was Studio Rivbe, owned by painter/musician Larry Rivers, where I saw unknown players as I sat on the floor and leaned against a bare wall.

One of my first long music pieces was about the loft jazz scene in Soho, which I penned for the *Amsterdam News*. I focused on a duo called Double Dark, a sax-and-drum combo composed of the magnificent reedman David Murray and the loquacious Stanley Crouch

My mother, Arizona, as a teenager in Newport News, Virginia, in the forties.

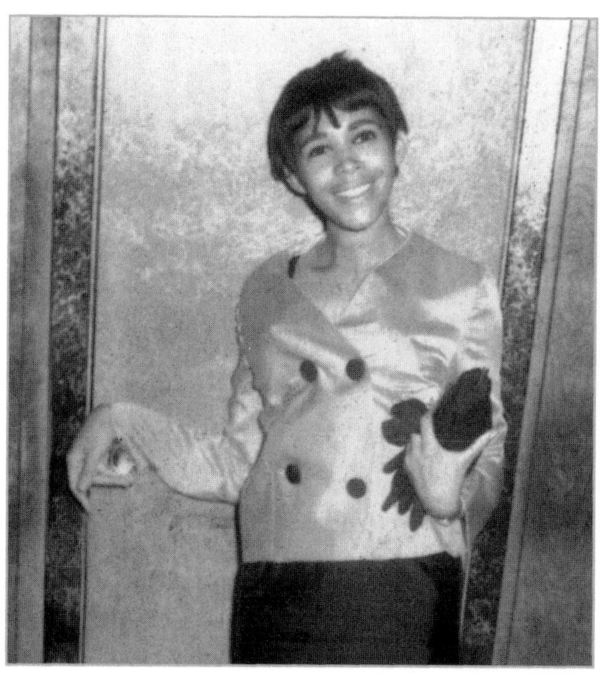

Arizona George as a young newlywed in Brooklyn, in the early sixties.

Andrea Patrice George and me, posing in our living room in the Tilden projects, 1960s.

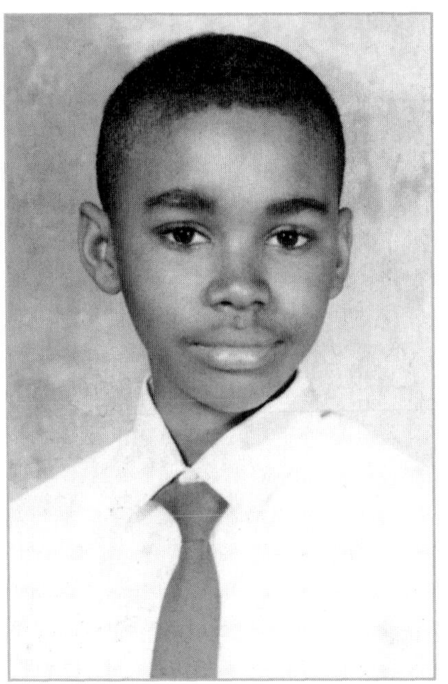

My P.S. 189 elementary school portrait.

Easter party at a community center at Ebbets Field in the mid-seventies.

Our first home outside the projects, 1081 New Jersey Avenue. We lived on the second floor, where my sister and I finally got our own bedrooms.

My first typewriter. The sports stars on the wall were soon replaced with music icons.

The *Amsterdam News* offices in Harlem, 1977.

The *Amsterdam News* newsroom. Les Matthews is on the right.

Still a freelancer at *Billboard*.

My desk at *Billboard*—we didn't get computers until the mid-eighties. Artists—like Grace Jones, here—dropped by regularly.

Outside the famous Motown studio on West Grand Boulevard in Detroit, 1985. I was researching my book on Motown.

Downstairs at Radio City Music Hall, where I got to interview one of my favorite singers, Anita Baker, for *Billboard*.

My mid-eighties publicity photo—from my Teddy Pendergrass phase.

The Beastie Boys opened for Madonna at Madison Square Garden in 1986. Their deejay, Rick Rubin, is the guy in the towel.

Arizona and my dad, Nelson Elmer, in Mom's backyard at 812 New Jersey Avenue, in the mid-eighties.

Andrea in front of the house in East New York. She's about twenty.

Fort Greene Park, 1988.

Eazy-E had a cameo in my movie *CB4*. We're on the set in Los Angeles here.

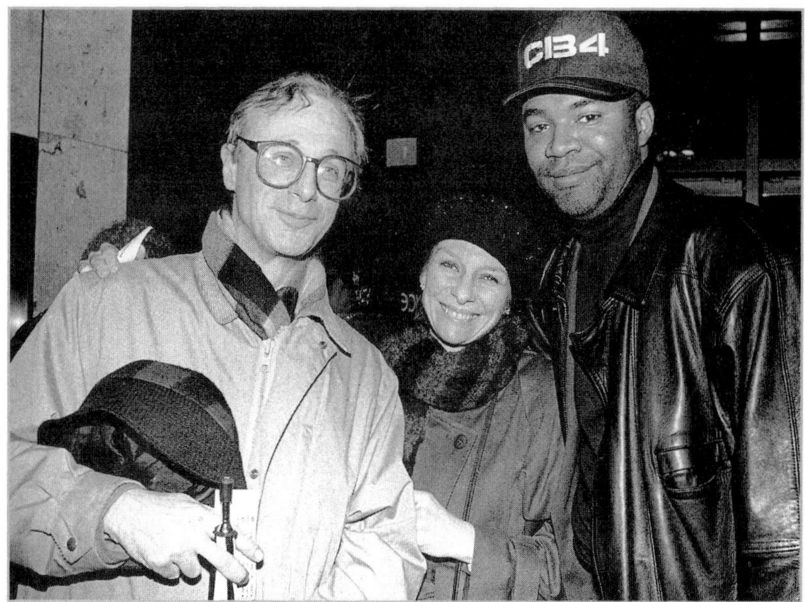

Bob Christgau, one of my mentors, and his wife, Carola Dibbell, at the premiere of *CB4* in Times Square, March 1993.

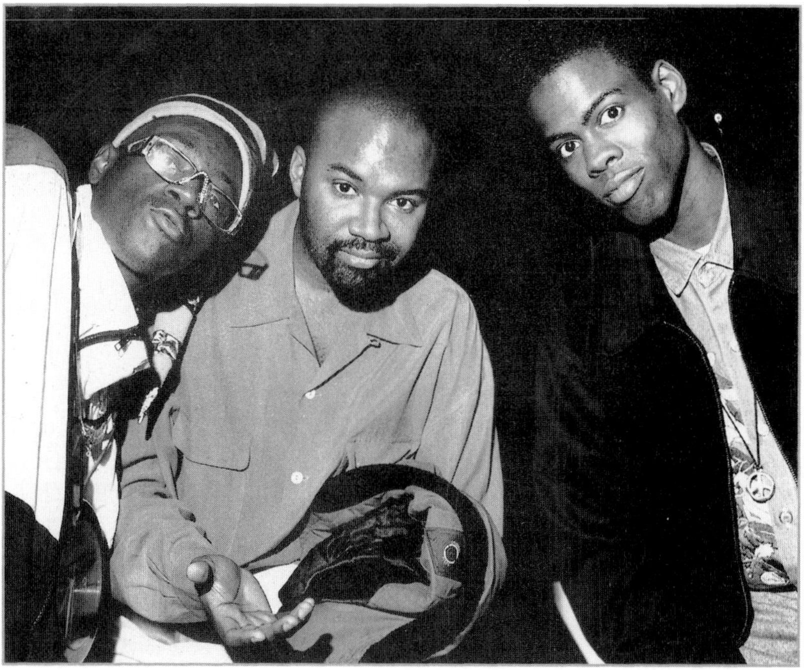

© suekwon

Flavor Flav, me, and young Chris Rock in Manhattan, early nineties.

All the girls in Mom's living room in Newport News—Andrea, Amber, Ebony, and Jade, with Arizona watching over them all.

Russell Simmons and me with our mutual mentor, Robert "Rocky" Ford, in 2003, at a screening of *Everyday People*.

That's me with President Barack Obama when he ran for the U.S. Senate in 2004.

The family comes together for Amber's high school graduation in 2003. Mom, me, Andrea, and Nelson Elmer.

on skins. Murray was a prodigious player of passion and skill, who'd go on to have a prolific career as a bandleader and composer. Less distinguished musically, but with a lot to say nonetheless, was Crouch, who'd already started writing for the *Voice*, and was booking bands at a Bowery club called the Tin Palace. Today Stanley is a pillar of jazz as the "American classical music" world, institutionalized inside the black reflecting glass of the TimeWarner building at Columbus Circle. But back then, sans the suits and the awards, he was a fixture in the avant-garde scene blossoming downtown.

For me, as for most folks then, Soho was very much a place to move through and not to linger in. The West Village—now that was a destination. In the summer, as it had been for generations, Washington Square Park was a gathering place for kids from all over the city, where you flirted with the opposite sex, bought drugs, joined the buskers leading sing-alongs, or checked out the comedians telling jokes by the fountain. The days of Bob Dylan and the folkies were long gone, but everyone was still turned on by the idea that he'd been there.

Then over to the basketball courts on Fourth Street and Sixth Avenue. In the days before multimillion-dollar contracts were common, NBA players, college stars, and street ball legends regularly risked life and limb in the summer league before crowds four deep on Sixth Avenue. Afterward I'd venture over to Eighth Street, where you got a gas-inducing hot dog at Orange Julius (where Russell Simmons found work one summer), and checked out the funky clothing stores or a movie at the Waverly Theater, where *The Rocky Horror Picture Show* made its original midnight run.

But winter or spring, especially during that period when my career was in peril, I'd venture over to Sheridan Square (past the already legendary Stonewall gay bar, and all manner of homoerotic clothing stores) to a downstairs bar/restaurant named the Lion's Head. I'd read about the Lion's Head in books about Norman Mailer and articles about an eccentric New York Giants fan, Frederick Exley, who'd penned a cult classic titled *Pages from a Cold Island.* The Head was a literary hangout, and I, a precocious wannabe, was drawn to it. So after J&R, the Greek spot, and a walk through Soho and the Village, I often ended up descending into the Lion's Head to feel the vibe.

Across from the bar, book jackets were hung like trophies. Mailer, Exley, and *Sports Illustrated* staffer Dan Jenkins were among the many names saluted there and envied by me. Many of the men and women bending elbows at the bar were real-life published authors. Too intimidated to hang at the bar, I'd sit in the back, usually at a table underneath a jauntily dressed frog in a red convertible.

Rolling Rock became my Lion's Head passion. It came in a round green bottle, and tasted cool and crisp in a way the Ballantine and Rheingold beer sold in Brooklyn never did. Going to the Lion's Head made me feel part of the larger writing world. Instead of pressing my face against the glass, I walked in and had a beer and a hamburger. I'm sure the regulars wondered who this skinny black kid was, since the crowd was as white as a politician's handkerchief. But the odd glances didn't bother me, especially after a couple of Rolling Rocks.

If I had enough money or, even better, was on a record company guest list, my last stop of the day was back across Fourth Street and Washington Square. The Bottom Line was where I, and generations of New Yorkers, kept up with the cutting edge of pop music throughout the eighties. From my college years through my retirement from full-time music criticism in 1989, I saw more music and experienced more life there than at any other venue in New York, including the Apollo and the Garden.

Even before Bruce Springsteen played his storied week of gigs there in 1976 and established his legend, the Bottom Line was already the top talent showcase in the city. If Warner Bros. or Columbia or RCA had a new band or singer who they wanted radio programmers, concert promoters, and magazine editors to know, they'd either headline or open at this modest cabaret. Really wasn't much to it. A long side bar, a cluttered little stage, and dark wood seats and tables, most of which were organized into tight, barely passable rows. The best seats were in the back and faced stage center, because the two thick columns often obscured side views. The food? Always awful, but since the labels usually picked up the tab, I ate a lot more of it than I should have.

Though it was no palace, the Bottom Line was my home away from home, a place I'd visit as many as four nights a week starting in 1980. There were so many gigs. There are so many memories. I got an education in the art of the backbeat from watching the Meters. I was moved by the surprising soul in the voice of the late Lowell George of Little Feat. I was frustrated watching Branford Marsalis play brilliant sax in front of a room of Japanese tourists, and then, two days later, seeing Kenny G play woefully for a sold-out show of worshipful African Americans. I happily caught Valerie Simpson's earring when it popped off her ear during an Ashford & Simpson show, and gave it to my date.

I was using these visits to write pulp magazine features and get free meals. My dream, however, was to contribute to the *Village Voice*'s Riffs section. At the Bottom Line I'd look into the back-row seats for Robert Christgau, who was, according to himself and others, the "dean" of American rock critics, figuring he was headmaster of the school I wanted admittance to.

Back in the seventies, when opinionated, visionary rock critics walked the earth, and celebrity journalism hadn't yet totally exterminated theoretical thinking in the pop press, I had begun reading the *Voice* music reviews, falling under the sway of Lester Bangs, Vince Aletti, and Christgau. Their ideas about music, and the connections made to the larger world I read about in the *Voice*, jibed with how I saw the world, though I hadn't figured out how to articulate it yet. Even as I sat out in the boondocks of Brooklyn, I was hoping there was more to reality than what I saw every day. The Riffs section, somehow, some way, confirmed that I was right.

I submitted my first reviews to Christgau and the *Voice* back in 1976, my first semester in college. It was about a big funk-soul concert at the Nassau Coliseum. Christgau wrote me a very nice rejection letter, full of criticism and condemnation that gave me hope. I sent two more reviews. With one came another typed letter, but after that two form letters followed, and, for a time, I licked my wounds.

During my year and a half in the freelance wilderness, now older and with some credits, I began calling Christgau whenever I could. Still no assignments were forthcoming. Far as I knew, only a few black writers had cracked the *Village Voice–Rolling Stone–Circus* magazine world of rock writing: Pablo Yoruba Guzmán, former Young Lord and future TV news reporter, and Vernon Gibbs, an erudite journalist and future A&R executive. Other than that, people of color were scarce on that circuit.

One night at the Bottom Line, I spotted Christgau and walked over. I knew what he looked like from a photo that accompanied a piece in the *Voice* on the rock criticism establishment of which he was "the Dean." His pale face was dominated by ever-present glasses and unruly hair that combined to make him look intense and unkempt, scholarly and judgmental. I stepped up to him about some work, and he told me, in what I'd later find out was his typically brusque but quite loving manner, "Nelson, you're not ready."

Lots of people would have taken that as an insult. Me? I just assumed he meant that eventually I would be ready. Maybe I was hearing what I wanted to hear. Still, I didn't take our meeting as a dis but as an opportunity. Christgau knew who I was. He knew my work. It was only a matter of time. Walking toward the subway at West Fourth Street for the long ride home to Queens, that's what I told myself.

KINGS FROM QUEENS

Queens was a bedroom I slept in more than a place I called home during my five years there. My professional life was in Manhattan, and my heart was still in Brooklyn, though my education as a critic continued in the home borough of the Mets. Combining the records of my roommate Rocky Ford and my collection, we easily had over two thousand disks, so I was always listening to new stuff and catching up on the old. For example, one night we got new albums by three of our favorites—Steely Dan's *Aja*, Stevie Wonder's *Hotter Than July*, and Earth, Wind & Fire's *All 'N' All*—and sat on our living-room floor analyzing the songs, arrangements, production, sound, even album graphics. Rocky, who was a budding producer, helped me hear music in a much more sophisticated manner in listening sessions that developed my ear and fueled my criticism.

It was while living in Queens that I was introduced to a soon to be great friend and sometime teacher. I don't remember when I first met Russell Simmons, but my first memory of him occurs in 1980, my first year living just off Parsons Boulevard in Jamaica. At that point Rocky was already working with Kurtis Blow, and Russell was acting as his manager, though Blow was more interested in having Rocky and his partner, J. B. Moore, handle his career. That was understandable, since he saw Rocky and J.B. as responsible adults, while he'd seen Russell, a City College classmate, doing angel dust in the student lounge.

I know I met Russell before but, for whatever reason, I didn't connect with him until one afternoon, when Rocky handed me the phone, exasperated with Russell's constant chatter. In fact, when I took the phone and identified myself, I don't believe Rush paused or shifted gears. As his nickname indicated, he just rushed on. I'd never heard anybody talk so fast who wasn't a cartoon character.

Russell was always excited, always enthused, and always selling, selling, selling. Though he's changed considerably in the three-plus decades I've known him, it's very rare that Russell isn't promoting something. There was a popular book back in the seventies called *The World's Greatest Salesman* by Og Mandino (a favorite of Michael Jackson), and, as far back as his twenties, Russell was a challenger for that crown.

That afternoon in 1980 Russell was rambling on about a party he was promoting to publicize one of Kurtis Blow's early singles, as if it was the most important gathering ever, a party so essential that everybody needed to be there for their own good. This ability to invest his words with a seductive urgency, to sell without a modicum of shame, drew me to him as it would scores of others.

From that phone call on, Russell was more than an irritant on the phone, but a great friend, though not a constant one; there would be gaps in our friendship, and many months when we didn't speak at all. Yet when I see him on the street, call or accept an unexpected invite to a party or show, it's like I saw him yesterday. I imagine it's like that for most of Russell's ever-expanding universe of best friends.

Russell was born about a month after me in 1957, and when we started hanging out we were both young men trying to make a mark. Russell gave me access to the art of selling a culture that I wouldn't have had otherwise. What Russell got from me, especially in those early days, when rap had few believers, was access to newspapers and magazines that spread his name and those of his clients. It never felt like a cut-and-dry trade, but this dimension of enlightened self-interest bonded us.

Despite our symbiotic relationship, many of my earliest memories of rolling with Rush involve being left behind. Working as a record promoter to club DJs to pay the bills, Russell was out every weekend and most weeknights. If you were "running the track" with him you'd get a serious education in dance music. The challenge was keeping up. Russell was notorious for entering clubs and either not telling the door person you were with him or seeing someone he wanted to "jock" (aka talk to) and forgetting about you. I found myself on the pavement quite a few times issuing the tired complaint "Yo, I'm with him!" from the bad side of a velvet rope.

In 1981 Kurtis Blow released his follow-up to "The Breaks," a single called "Throughout Your Years," which was Rocky and J. B. Moore's attempt at crafting another pop crossover single. To promote it in Queens and Long Island, Russell booked the MC into four clubs on one night, so he'd do a short set, and, with Russell and some roadies, pile into a van to hit the next spot. I was tagging along one night, 'cause I had a girl in Hempstead I wanted to see. We hooked up at the club, went outside to her car, which had a roomy backseat, and got busy. Before I left the club I told Russell, no matter what, don't leave without me. Maybe I stayed too long.

Maybe he just forgot about me. Either way, the van was gone when I got back to the club, and I spent a long night curled up on a Long Island Rail Road bench, having missed the night's last train back to New York.

If you managed to get in the club with Russell, and also managed to stay close to him, you gained entry, not simply to a disco but to a network of strange relationships. At that time there was a lot of racial/cultural segregation in New York music circles, where Euro disco, funk, punk, and glitzy R&B all existed in separate worlds. Through his record promotion gig, and his own careerism and curiosity, Russell sampled them all. Sure, he hit the hip-hop spots in the South Bronx, Harlem, and Queens, but he also cultivated relationships at punk rock and new wave clubs like Hurrah's and the Peppermint Lounge, as well as black upscale Midtown hangouts like Leviticus and Othello's.

While Russell and I were close, the budding mogul wasn't my only entry to the world of hip-hop. There were players on the scene then, mostly people who either couldn't make the leap as hip-hop reached the next level, or dropped out too soon. I went to clubs and concerts in Queens, the Bronx, and Harlem that were still called "discos," but which we'd now identify as "hip-hop."

Wherever I ventured in those pioneering days, I had the same feeling over and over. There was a mix of fear and freedom at the early rap shows that made me feel totally alive, as if I could die at any moment or experience a rush of joyous adrenaline. And since I'm still alive, despite being present at several shootings and more fistfights than I could count, it worked out for me. That heady mix of violence and exhilaration followed me from parties at Harlem nightclubs to arena shows at Madison Square Garden. For me rap shows walked on the edge of chaos, and could be tipped over and back several times a night.

The first time I saw hip-hop music performed before thousands of people was at the City College of New York gym in 1978. (About ten years later it was the site of a fatal stampede at a Puff Daddy–promoted event.) The show was billed as an R&B concert with Harold Melvin & the Blue Notes (minus Teddy Pendergrass), an unheralded funk band named Brainstorm, and Philly's teenaged disco-soul singer Evelyn "Champagne" King. But set up on the far right side of the stage were two turntables where D. J. Hollywood and Lovebug Starski held forth between sets.

With Starski cutting on the ones and twos, Hollywood, a heavy-set young man with oodles of charisma and a booming low tenor voice, rhymed over beats like Earth, Wind & Fire's "Brazilian Rhyme." It was my first time hearing "throw your hands in the air and wave 'em like you just don't care," and other, then fresh, now cliché party phrases. The young uptown crowd knew every bit of Hollywood's show, chanting along and responding to him as if he was yanking them by their gold chains. Must have been two thousand young people enthralled with these beats and his rhymes in a way none of the R&B stars could match.

If that was the only revelation of my first R&B versus rap moment, it would have been memorable. But something else was going on. Three times during that evening, fights broke out. I was sitting in the bleachers stage left. Below me on the gym floor were hundreds of metal chairs. Several times people down on the gym floor would shout, blows would be hurled, and chairs would go flying. In a prescient echo of the later CCNY tragedy, pandemonium would reign. Then the violence would subside, and the fight/robbery would end (for the moment), and everyone would return to their seats, and Hollywood, undaunted and surely used to such drama, would rock the mike again.

This will to party, even in the face of obvious danger, was something I'd witness over and over in those early shows. The next big hip-hop event I attended was the Sugarhill Convention held at the Harlem Armory. It was 1981, and rap records were becoming the hottest items uptown. On the bill were Grandmaster Flash and the Furious Five, the Treacherous Three, and several other uptown icons. I was there with two hip-hop tourists—Guy Trebay, a columnist for the *Village Voice* (where I was finally freelancing), and a very comely, light-skinned single lady I'll call Alma, who worked in the *Voice*'s art department.

The stage was on the floor of the cavernous armory, with most attendees standing on the floor in front of the stage. After my CCNY experience there was no way I was gonna be on that floor. So I guided Guy and Alma up to a balcony that overlooked the floor. From there we could see hundreds of young people milling about, flirting and dancing the Patty Duke along with several other then popular dances. As the music flowed, we could look down and see little clumps of people, mostly boys, move through the crowd, bumping into people and causing little testosterone-fueled dustups. Then, like a tossed rock rippling through a pond, the crowd would part, as weapons were drawn. Two or three people would scrap. The battle would subside. The music played. After this happened two or three times, Alma praised my good judgment for sitting us upstairs.

Down below, the scrapping escalated. A gun was pulled. A shot was fired. The crowd scattered, and fear infected everyone like a dope beat. This was a time before crack, so gunplay like this still wasn't commonplace. I grabbed Alma's hand and Alma grabbed Guy's. Somehow we moved through the crowd, down a long staircase, and out into the street without stumbling, or being stomped or robbed. I was really worried about Guy, a tall, whiter-than-white man in glasses. He would be an easy target in the chaos, but he was cool and collected, and we made it out of there safely. The theme remained the same throughout the eighties: energetic crowd, cutting-edge music, random violence.

I remember feeling the same restlessness, palpable anger, and intense enthusiasm at every show I attended during the eighties. But I must admit that feeling that something could jump off at any moment was actually part of the attraction. This wasn't "rap violence," as the tabloids labeled it. Just because something happened in a club or concert hall didn't make it any different from the violence that was escalating in the streets.

The same stick-up kids and gangsta wannabes who were squeezing off in the streets outside the concert halls brought that attitude inside. These hip-hop gigs were the perfect cover. In the darkness of a club or arena, with innocent eyes peering toward the stage, the criminal-minded could run up on a victim unseen and, because of the music, unheard. This was especially true if the venue had a standing-room-only section or wide aisles between the chairs on the arena floor.

As a rule I never took floor seats at rap shows. I'd sit on the sides or in the mezzanine, so I could see the stage better. If forced to be in the standing sections, I'd spend a lot of the show watching my back, just in case a bum's rush was imminent. By the time hip-hop was playing arenas, Russell's Rush Management was booking most of the shows, so I went to a great many of them, feeling that same sense of exhilaration and dread on many nights.

Truth be told, I actually miss that feeling. So many of the major rap shows I've been to in the twenty-first century feel like boxing exhibitions, not real fights. You never feel like you're gonna see anything new, or that anyone in the crowd is risking anything, and I'm including the fans. The crowds can be as complacent as the music, meaning that if they receive a crappy show (and they often do), they take it passively, and then head home quietly.

At the end of 1980 I was called in by *Record World* magazine, then *Billboard*'s chief competition, for a job interview. The work I'd done in college at *Billboard* had not gone unnoticed. They were looking to hire a new black music editor, and my experience in trade reporting made me the prime candidate. In January 1981, I started the first and, subsequently, only nine-to-five job of my life. Celebrating his friend's ascendance, Russell threw me a congratulatory party at, of all places, the buppie disco Leviticus. The black-owned disco that had dissed (and would continue to dis) younger people throughout the eighties was where Russell introduced me to the record business establishment. I remember my mother sipping a piña colada that night, proud to see her "shining black prince" making the name Nelson George mean something in the world.

At *Record World* I began integrating coverage of hip-hop culture into stories on the Gap Band, Shalamar, etc. From that platform I began writing better paying freelance pieces, including my first for the *Village Voice*—two short reviews of rap 12-inch singles, one by Lovebug Starski on Harlem World Records, and Grandmaster Flash and the Furious Five's "The Great Adventures of Grandmaster Flash on the Wheels of Steel." For *Record World* I worked on a very comprehensive Sugar Hill Records advertorial that in its gate-fold section printed every word of the Sugarhill Gang's thirteen-minute "Rapper's Delight."

I've been credited a few places for helping to invent hip-hop journalism. My only goal back then was, in fact, the opposite—to weave hip-hop in with the other, more established black music styles I was covering. At that time this struck quite a few people as radical. Many saw hip-hop as a disreputable break from the traditions of the past, when it was really just an evolution that was more connected to black music's traditions than they could see. The dress and language of the day scared folks off. So did the fact that most MCs, and even many of their early producers, couldn't play any traditional instruments. Yet the young people who created hip-hop actually loved the traditions. They just found their own way of honoring them.

One of my most vivid memories of that period, one that illustrates my point perfectly, comes from Madison Square Garden in '82. In one of the oddest concert lineups in history, Kurtis Blow opened for the Commodores and Bob Marley and the Wailers. Marley, though already a headline act in the United States, took the gig in an attempt to reach out to African Americans who hadn't been as into reggae as whites.

I helped Davey D carry some of his equipment onstage, and then looked out at the weird mix of Rastafarians, buppies, and pop music fans who filled the Garden. This was as culturally diverse a crowd as you could imagine, and Blow rocked them. The Rastas responded to Blow like he was U-Roy or another reggae "toasting" DJ. The Commodores' crowd dug the R&B beats and enjoyed "throwing their hands in the air and waving" like they just didn't care.

While both the Rastas and the R&B folk accepted Kurtis Blow, this kind of musical fellowship didn't extend at all to the headliners. After a typically soulful Marley set (I was honored to have seen the Wailers three times before this), most of Bob's crowd got up and left when Lionel Richie began tinkling on the ivories to play "Still" and "Three Times a Lady." The gap between crossover black pop and reggae back then was an ocean, but a hip-hop DJ and MC easily crossed that water.

The success of Blow, Run-D.M.C., and the growing visibility of hip-hop would alter the direction of everyone in our circle of friends. It put Russell on a hedonistic path he'd stay on, nonstop, for another decade. Our good buddy and former Def Jam executive Bill Stephney used to call him "Spuds MacKenzie," after the bull terrier who became the party animal symbol of Bud Lite. Already a creature of the night from his life as a record promoter, Russell became the man who either produced or released the records played by the club jocks, emerging as a significant figure in New York nightlife, a role he fulfilled with gusto.

Hip-hop's emergence changed my career direction as well. First at *Record World*, and then at *Billboard* magazine, I became a middleman between the established world of rhythm and blues and the still relatively underground world of rap music. I was writing about the Fat Boys and Tommy Boy Records alongside major label releases and records by the likes of Jermaine Jackson and Patti LaBelle. There wasn't yet a media infrastructure to support this culture. So it was me and a few other young journalists who, while not necessarily crusading for hip-hop, worked to normalize it for the reluctant old heads in the record industry and the media. Young record buyers didn't need us necessarily, since they were finding (and defining) what a hot rap record was quite nicely on their own.

In 1985, I wrote a long profile of Russell for the *Village Voice*. Rush Management, at that moment, represented most of the biggest names in rap, and promoted tours with the rest of them. In a little two-room office on Broadway in the Twenties, Russell and his small staff had business relationships with everyone who mattered in the rap game at that time. The piece, which closely followed a *Wall Street Journal* article that labeled him "the mogul of rap," helped project Russell as a personality to the *Voice*'s multiracial, music-savvy readership. It was another red flag for mainstream media that rap in general, and Russell in particular, was a story worth covering.

It was the first of many large pieces I'd write for the *Voice*, which became my literary home during the amazing eighties. The Russell profile, in my mind, was the beginning of a new era for both of us. We were no longer young guys desperately trying to get into the mix. We had kinda arrived. People knew we had something to offer. We weren't proven yet, but we were on people's radar screen. Which meant, to me, that it was time to get the hell out of Queens.

BLACK HOLLYWOOD

Although I am a Brooklyn boy through and through, many of my most important personal relationships and lucrative professional achievements occurred in Los Angeles, California. I've spent more time in the city of lost angels than in any place other than New York. It's where I learned the joys of nasty hotel sex. It's where I've made the largest sums of money. Even my most commercially successful novel, *One Woman Short*, was set out there. I know parts of LA better than I do areas in Brooklyn, which is strange, since I never learned to drive, but if driven somewhere, I rarely forget how I got there.

My first trip west was in 1981 to attend the Black Music Association conference at the Century City Hotel. On the way in from LAX, I got sick in the taxi, which happened on my first five trips to California (including on a journey to San Francisco to interview Marvin Gaye). My sinuses had been finicky since I was seven. I'd regularly weathered migraine headaches when there were radical temperature changes or on days of high pollen.

But I'd never felt worse than in the taxi that day. My head hurt. I felt nauseous. Between my first transcontinental plane trip and LA's smoggy air, I was wasted. After checking in I had to lie down with a wet cloth on my forehead. Not a great intro to Cali.

When I finally got myself together, I ventured down to the lobby, and couldn't help but marvel at the number of scantily clad women lounging around, sometimes alone, but usually in groups of twos and threes. In teased hair, pumps, and extreme eighties makeup, they watched me as intently as I eyed them. Some were hookers. A bunch were groupies, hoping to hook up with an R&B star. A few were actually well-trained singers trying to attract the attention of a producer or record exec. These distinctions were lost on me at first. It just looked like the sexy California dream to me.

Pumped up on antihistamines and determined to overcome jet lag, I shared a taxi to Hollywood with my Queens roommate Rocky Ford, and went to a press party at Yamashiro's, a Japanese restaurant with a commanding view of LA. It was my first vision of the city at night, with its thousands of twinkling stars spread out as far as the eye could see. I downed free sushi and chatted with radio DJs, record executives, and wannabe stars. I ran into a friend from New York, Randy Muller, who produced hits for Brass Construction and Skky. Along with Rocky and Randy, I walked down the hill from Yamashiro's to Hollywood Boulevard. It was my first time on this legendary street, and it didn't disappoint.

Cars jammed the street, cruising slowly in a California ritual, many with their tops down. And car after passing car was blasting Rick James's "Give It to Me Baby." Where in New York disco and hip-hop flowed from ghetto blasters, in Cali souped-up sound systems filled the night air with punk funk. Girls in halter tops tossed their phone numbers to guys in passing sports cars. It felt like a scene from an urban version of *American Graffiti,* where black and Chicano kids had replaced their white counterparts, and lowriders were the car to have.

It felt right that my first taste of LA nightlife had a Motown soundtrack. Ten years after its move from Detroit to the West Coast, the black pop culture of Tinseltown was still very defined by its presence. The Jacksons, the Gordys, other offspring of the Motown universe, and their friends constituted a kind of black showbiz royalty. If you went to a club or a concert out there, it was the Motowners who got the best seats and had the most juice.

By moving to LA, Motown had shifted the nexus of mainstream black entertainment out there, and inspired many local initiators (Dick Griffey's SOLAR Records, Lonnie Simmons's Total Experience). The Motown model of success was the template. At Sunset off Vine was the Motown Building, perhaps the only large structure in the city that carried the name of a black-owned business. One long block away on Gower was Roscoe's House of Chicken 'n Waffles, a black institution, where anybody and everybody in black pop culture came through for the house specialty of four chicken wings and two waffles.

Though I couldn't drive, and hated paying LA's inflated taxi fees, I'd drag my ass over to Roscoe's on every trip I made to Cali during my days as a music journalist. I'd set up back-to-back meetings there, interview folks, and then linger around to see who'd run through. A long afternoon at Roscoe's would fill up my *Billboard* column for at least two weeks.

While the cream of the city's black middle class lived in Baldwin Hills, View Park, and Ladera Heights, the growing black Hollywood community favored predictable white enclaves like Beverly Hills, Westwood, and Brentwood, and San Fernando Valley towns like Encino, where the Jackson clan was based.

The amount of money that black Hollywood had (or was it the

flashy way they spent it?) always knocked me out. I became friendly with a smart, young black A&R dude out there named John. He was plugged into the young Motown crowd, but had landed a job at a rival label, where he'd go on to develop a major young black female pop star. He had crazy sports cars, a pad in Westwood that looked like the set from *American Gigolo,* and a taste for superexpensive clothes. I rolled with him one afternoon to a Beverly Hills boutique, where he dropped about ten grand on clothes. When he offered to treat me to a fifteen-hundred-dollar sweater, I passed, but it shocked me how cavalier he was about his cash.

Coming from the hard streets of BK, the LA lifestyle was a serious culture shock for me. I knew there were gangs in LA, and hardworking folks scrambling to make it. But my initial eighties experiences out there had a lot more to do with Fred Siegel's boutique on Melrose than with Bloods and Crips. This was the era of Michael Jackson and Lionel Richie, a time when black pop was about being as mainstream as could be.

I was kind of a curiosity to the folks I met out there. They read me, first at *Record World* and then at *Billboard,* on a weekly basis. They always thought I was older than I looked. I think they were amused by my fascination/disdain with how they handled their money and their smooth vibe of entitlement. I recall spending a long afternoon with Quincy Jones at his Bel Air home. Q was, and remains, the most charming man I've ever met. You spend five minutes with him, and you realize why he's been able to work successfully with so many artists. You immediately want to please him, because he really put you at ease.

We had lunch, and I asked for some apple juice. Well, his cook brought out a glass of freshly squeezed apple juice. I was stunned.

I mean, damn, they actually ground up the apple in the kitchen. It says a lot about how limited my experience with healthy eating was at that time that, now, decades later, I can still clearly see that glass of pulpy juice being placed in front of me. Quincy, who I am sure was amused by my reaction, just smiled, probably having introduced scores of young black folks to "the good life" over the years.

At one point I asked Q what separated the great stars from the near greats he'd worked with. "Ass power" was his reply. To illustrate his point, Q compared Michael Jackson to another well-known vocalist he'd produced. The other singer, an artist with an immense voice and an insatiable appetite for cocaine, would come to the studio, maybe lay down a scratch vocal, and then wander off for hours. Jackson, in contrast, would come to the studio, record a strong lead vocal, work on the stacked vocal harmonies that distinguished his work, and practice where to place those ad-libs that were his trademark.

"His ass power," Q said, "would keep him in the studio until he felt he'd accomplished something that day. That ability to focus, to stay in that chair in the studio, listening to playback and then going back in to record some more—that's what separates the good from the great."

From then on, "ass power" became an integral part of my vocabulary. I invoked it whenever I had a deadline to meet or was encouraging friends in their efforts. If "ass power" was what Quincy Jones and Michael Jackson used to record masterful music, I needed a bit myself.

At the end of a long, beautiful interview about everyone from Frank Sinatra to Dinah Washington, I was sitting with Q in his living room when a tall, willowy, Swedish blonde appeared. She was a young actress/model/singer who looked a lot like one of Q's ex-wives. Felt like this was a cue to call a taxi. Instead he told me to stay. We sat on a sofa, and the young woman sat on the floor before us, holding up her portfolio of photos for us to peruse. At the time, I'd never really contemplated dating a white woman, and certainly never kissed one, so it was crazy watching her down at my feet. Q, of course, took it all in stride.

If that wasn't enough, Q told the blonde that she needed to have dinner with me that night. And she agreed. Q winked at me, and I got the hell out of there. That night I sat with the young lady at a Sunset Boulevard hot spot, Carlos 'n Charlie's, a restaurant with a popular upstairs disco. I was way out of my league with this lady. Aside from being "friends" with Q, she was already friends with the actor/musician Dudley Moore and a few other high-profile gents.

Nothing went down between the blonde and me, but the day with Q did crystallize the black eighties Hollywood experience for me. If you could push and claw yourself into the LA celebrity machine, you could live a lifestyle unmatched by any previous generation of blacks. The money was there. The women were available. There were more opportunities emerging throughout the decade.

Yet I was unsure if all this was for me. I was a bookish guy, more scholar than player, more observer than hustler. My obsessions had more to do with knowledge than power. Still, LA tugged at me, like the Hyde side of Dr. Jekyll, and I've always wondered what would happen if I gave in to its pull.

FROM MOTOROLA TO MOTOWN

As I noted earlier, my mother's Motorola played a huge role in my life. Moreover, like so many who'd been reared on the sixties' music, I was fascinated with the Motown sound. Like all black folks, I'd read studiously about Berry Gordy, Diana Ross, and all the label's other stars in *Ebony* and *Jet*. As I grew older, graduating to more serious music mags, like *Rolling Stone* and *Circus*, my interest in how this black institution had conquered the music world intensified. I had tons of questions about how and why it worked, and very few satisfying answers. There were useful articles here and there. Most of the best had been published in UK publications like *Black Music*.

But there was no single book that told the whole story and sated my curiosity. So when I was seventeen or eighteen I decided I'd write the book I wanted to read, and I kept that goal in mind all through my struggling freelance days, and into my years at *Billboard*. I'd always been a pack rat (a habit I picked up from my mother), clipping items from newspapers, making little notes in black and white composition books.

I'd interview Smokey Robinson for a story on "Being with You," or Diana Ross for a piece on her RCA hit "Why Do Fools Fall in Love," or Lionel Richie about his success with ballads, and I'd always make sure I slipped in questions about the label's 1960s peak and seventies transformation, looking for a fresh tidbit or confirmation of an oft-told tale. Even *The Michael Jackson Story,* my first book, a paperback quickie I wrote in a furious two months in summer '83, was in my mind really just an excuse to dig for Motown gold and make some much-needed cash.

As I talked to old R&B heads who'd been around when Joe and Katherine Jackson brought their brood from Gary, Indiana, to Detroit, I actually became more interested in the world they had entered into by joining Motown than with the headlining family itself. I'd been writing regularly for *Musician* magazine, so in 1983 I pitched them a profile of the Motown session men. Except for the names of legendary bassist James Jamerson and drummer Benny Benjamin, the session players behind the hits were faceless. They were often praised by the singers but rarely by name, whereas producers like Holland-Dozier-Holland, Norman Whitfield, and Smokey had a near mythic status.

Unlike Booker T & the MGs (the Memphis Group) or Philly's MFSB, the Motown session cats didn't have catchy handles. Hidden behind the Motown marketing machine, they were as obscure as an old-time Delta bluesman to even dedicated music fans. Through my contacts among musicians I was able to run down a phone number for Anne Jamerson, the wife of James. I'd heard Jamerson was gravely ill. To my surprise, Anne thought it was a great idea for her husband to talk with me, and put me in contact with him at a hospital in California. From what she told me, medication had messed with his ability to play and sent him into a depression. Others suggested he'd suffered from drug and alcohol abuse brought on by the loss of the support system he'd had back in Detroit.

I wasn't allowed to go see him, but she set up a phone call on a Sunday afternoon. His voice was weak and weary, and his tone bittersweet. He guided me through sessions, told me the studio group's nickname, the Funk Brothers, and gave me the kind of sensual detail about the making of Motown's hits that had been lacking in interviews with the producers and artists over the years. He related that his works were inspired by life, noting, for example, that the percolating riff that anchored "Standing in the Shadows of Love" came from watching the hips of a woman strolling down a Detroit avenue.

For me it was a revelatory experience, putting me close to the creation of the sounds that had flowed from Ma's Motorola. As crucial as that conversation was, it was just a gateway to a world that could only truly be explored by trips to one of the most vilified cities in America—Detroit, Michigan.

In the early eighties the nighttime streets of downtown Detroit were empty, save the occasional tumbleweed sighting by Cobo Hall. Okay, I exaggerate, but not a whole lot. Aside from the nights Cobo filled with suburban Red Wing fans (many from across the border in Canada), or for a concert, pedestrians were scarce. Sometimes even cars, the spine and pride of the Motor City, could be few and far between.

Between the 1967 riots and its early eighties notoriety as the United States' murder capital, not much had gone right in Detroit. Its anemic downtown nightlife was just one of the results. In fact, even during the day Detroit didn't resemble Chicago or Boston.

But to be walking through Detroit at night must have seemed particularly foolhardy to the locals. Yet there I was, in a brown leather jacket and wool cap, armed only with a notebook, seeking one of the city's remaining musical oases.

Slipped in between the empty streets and the haunted avenues were clubs and bars where nocturnal culture still thrived. I'd enter and be met by the sound of jazz, and on the bandstand, playing for a middle-aged crowd, would be the men who made the Motown sound. You'd see pianist Earl Van Dyke or Johnny Griffith tapping ivories on "Green Dolphin Street"; Uriel Jones or Pistol Allen using brushes on "Stella by Starlight." No matter that they'd played on scores of pop anthems, at heart they'd been jazzmen, and, since these gigs were as much for their pleasure as for money, it's jazzmen they remained.

But I didn't just go to Detroit to see the players. Wrapped around the Motown sound was a network of workers, the people who on a daily basis executed Berry Gordy's vision, and you'd see them at these clubs as well. Motown Records left Detroit in 1972, but the fellowship the company had engendered was still palpable.

So was their bitterness. No matter how wonderful the memories of individual moments were, the overall tone of those who remained behind was tart, like the taste of a lemon had replaced that of an orange. The longer you talked to these men and women (all the musicians were male) you understood that the ex-Motowners shared the same sense of abandonment that filled the city itself.

My conversation with Jamerson and the publication of the *Musician* article (titled "Standing in the Shadows of Motown") gave me entrée to the community of players and employees in Detroit, and encouraged me to keep pursuing this dream. It also let some of the label's highly protective representatives know I was digging around in uncharted territory. As a result, I was supported by those no longer associated with Motown, and faced harassment from folks who currently worked there.

Several people, including a girlfriend, asked me why I would even attempt such an undertaking. I'd asked this young lady, who was attending law school, to look over some of the Motown contracts and let me know whether they looked as abusive as some artists contended. Instead, she gave me a lecture on leaving black institutions alone, that I shouldn't be negative. So I asked her to leave my apartment and never spoke to her again. I was on a mission now. I couldn't have that "negative" energy around me.

Moreover, the musicians wanted me to do it. All the great players left in Detroit, and the others I spoke to on either coast, wanted their story told. They were part of history too, yet they'd been left out. Most of these men were old enough to be my father, a couple could have been my grandfather, and that connection drew me to them as well. One of the pleasures of being in journalism is the time you get to spend with people you'd otherwise never meet. These Motown musicians had had full lives, lives that enriched the music and made them great storytellers.

I learned a lot about perseverance and patience from them, and about the beauty of collaboration. Learning to mesh your talents with the skills of other gifted people is a glorious thing. It's not easy to learn and very difficult to sustain. At this time I was very much a lone wolf when it came to work. I listened to my editors. I took advice here and there. But I usually kept my own counsel. I debated myself in my notebooks, but didn't let too many people, be they friend or lover, into my creative process. I didn't know it then, but these genius musicians would, by lesson and example, teach me how to work well with other artists, something that would filter into my filmmaking years later.

Visiting 2648 West Grand Boulevard, the original home of Motown Records, was a revelation. For all its mystique and history, this legendary building is just a nice two-story home on a quiet midwestern street. Its staircases are narrow, and you wonder how the long-limbed Temptations and Four Tops made it up and down them. The famous studio, site of the Motown sound, was an expanded basement, big by East Coast standards, perhaps, but in no way exceptional. The smallness of the place made what was achieved there all the more impressive.

That building on Detroit's West Grand Boulevard is an object lesson that world-changing events are so often created by small groups of like-minded individuals. Almost all major artistic movements (and most political as well) come out of small communities of folks linked by geography and shared values. Often they are based in seemingly unlikely places—Seattle or the South Bronx or Detroit—that only afterward seem like the perfect place for something new to burst out of.

Being at 2648 West Grand didn't make it nostalgic as much as it opened me up to the richness of the possibilities around me. What this community of black folks accomplished out of a house in Detroit was amazing, but it wasn't out of reach for other generations—my generation—to achieve in their own way, on their own terms.

It's not well remembered now, in our gangsta-celebrating era, that Motown suffered from an unsavory reputation dating back to the 1960s. Rumors floated around showbiz circles for years that Motown was actually owned not by Berry Gordy but by underworld figures. In my research (and in others') those rumors have never been substantiated. However, there's no doubt in my mind that Berry had some Detroit bad boys in his employ over the years.

As word of my book filtered out, I was subjected to different pressures from Motown loyalists. The most graphic example of harassment was at a Motown-produced TV special taped at the Apollo Theater in the early eighties. I was told I'd be denied access to the theater, the press viewing area, and the gala after-party behind the Apollo in a tent on 126th Street. Just to be contrary, I hung outside the press area, set up in a nearby school, and sneaked in carrying a TV camera to obscure my face. Then I was spotted by a member of Motown's publicity staff, who had security escort me out. Later, I slipped into the after-party, where I had a brief, funny conversation with Bobby Brown.

That veiled gangster mystique played a huge role in eliminating my chief competitor in chronicling Motown's history. A hot young white music critic had landed a book deal about the same time as I, and, in fact, had made contact with many of the same interview subjects, plus a few I hadn't gotten to yet.

So I was quite surprised when he asked me to meet him at an Upper West Side restaurant. I'll never forget that day, both because of the bizarre tale he told and because he gave me a clear lane to finish my book. The writer related that he'd received threats for "asking too many questions" by an ex-Motown executive. Yet what really freaked him out was a phone call he received after a trip to Detroit.

He claimed that a male voice told him, "We know where you live," as a helicopter appeared outside his Riverside Drive apartment window and hovered menacingly outside. To the writer this strange occurrence (if it happened as he described) meant, stay out of Detroit and drop this book. The idea that someone might have threatened him didn't seem far-fetched. Detroit was, after all, murder capital USA.

Ultimately, whether this was a paranoid fantasy or some incredible bit of staged intimidation, I didn't really care. Not only was he going to stop working on a rival Motown book, but he would sell me all his research. A deal was struck, and boxes of interviews and other materials joined the stack in my bedroom. Looking through the writer's interviews and notes, I realized his mistake. Number one, he had been quite blunt in asking for information about any Motown/Mob connections, as if they'd just spill whatever they knew simply because he asked them.

Moreover, he was a New York City white man interviewing mostly working-class black Midwesterners, and hadn't worked hard enough to dampen their natural suspicion. There was no doubt that the thrust of his interviews had gotten back to certain individuals in Detroit, who decided to test him. But a helicopter hovering over Riverside Drive? Still don't know what to make of that.

When I returned to Detroit I tried to push this writer's fear out of my mind. But one night, alone in my Renaissance Center Hotel room, I had a freak-out, worried that some hit man would break into my room, smack me around, and steal my interview tapes. I placed a chair under the doorknob, crumpled up newspapers on the floor, and talked animatedly on the phone to friends in New York until near dawn.

The paranoia passed, due largely to the fellowship of two men—longtime Motown keyboardist and bandleader Earl Van Dyke and musician and talent manager "Beans" Boles. Van Dyke was a tough, no-bullshit, brown-skinned man, with no illusions about the humanity of showbiz executives and the warmth of his fellow man. I recall driving with him through Detroit on two occasions when he pulled out his revolver and placed it on the seat of his car, because someone had cruised behind him a little too close. Some of the best observations in my book *Where Did Our Love Go?*, about Marvin Gaye's inner demons, Diana Ross's temperament, and Stevie Wonder's artistic development, came from Earl.

Beans Boles was a jovial, lean, light-skinned man, with great empathy for others, who walked me through the byzantine ways of the Motown business. While he joined Motown as saxophonist, Beans quickly became part of Motown's permanent government, working in their management, helping to book and run tours, and wrangling talent. In that capacity Beans dealt with all levels of the Motown hierarchy, including Berry, and key administrators.

Moreover, he generously gave me access to touring schedules, internal memos, and the notorious Motown contracts. But Beans didn't just give me access to the mechanics of the company, he opened up its soul, too, with very acute portraits of Marvin Gaye, Diana Ross, and sad Florence Ballard. Though the film *Dreamgirls* was fun, and gave a lot of young black talent a showcase, the real story of Motown was much more complex and nuanced than the film suggests, and it was through these fine men that I came to understand it.

Both Earl and Beans treated me warmly, and almost single-handedly guided me to all of the wonderful Motown musicians.

They gave me the confidence to believe I could finish the book, and, crucially, it was important to them that I did. Maybe because I wasn't close to my father, and I didn't know my grandfathers very well, I always enjoyed the fellowship of older black men. I never just tolerated them like some young people do. I genuinely enjoyed hearing their stories, not just for information, but for the closeness it engendered. My strongest memory of writing *Where Did Our Love Go?* is sitting in my Detroit hotel room, a bottle of Scotch and my tape recorder handy, listening to middle-aged black men tell the stories that no one else wanted to hear.

Flash forward: It's 2003, some twenty years after I seriously began researching my book, and I'm sitting in the Magno screening room in Midtown Manhattan about to watch a documentary about those great Motown musicians. *Standing in the Shadows of Motown* even carried the title of my long-ago *Musician* magazine profile. But watching the doc wasn't the pleasant experience of nostalgia I'd anticipated; instead, it brought me face-to-face with mortality.

About midway through that viewing I got choked up. But it wasn't until the penultimate sequence, when the remaining Funk Brothers came out carrying their instruments and photos of their fallen comrades, that I started crying like a baby.

I got up out of my seat and went into the men's room, where I tried to hide the tracks of my tears. The movie brought me back to 1983, '84, and '85, when I began to venture out to Detroit, Michigan, in search not simply of Motown Records' history, but of a piece of my childhood, and those moments when Jamerson's bass pumped against my chest through my mother's Motorola hi-fi. All my emotions mixed together: the joy of the music in my family's living room; the experience of being schooled on music and life by that feisty, funny group of musicians in Detroit; the challenge of writing my first book; and the reality that while the music lives on, eras pass and people die, often alone and overlooked. Deep inside me all the passion at that time in my life lives on, and I still feel it whenever one of those classic Motown singles comes on.

FORT GREENE DREAMS

In spring 1985 I was awakened in my Jamaica, Queens, apartment by a phone call from a young filmmaker I'd recently befriended. His high-pitched voice filled my ear.

"Nelson, this is Spike! Loved your piece on Russell Simmons in the *Voice*!"

He was referring to my profile of Rush that had run in April of that year. I thanked him, and we chatted. I told him I was moving to Brooklyn, to an area called Fort Greene.

"That's where I live!" he told me excitedly. Turned out I was moving right around the corner from him. I didn't know it at the time, but the publication of the Simmons profile, and moving from Queens to Fort Greene, was the end and beginning of two eras for me.

Moving from my Queens apartment with Rocky took me out of daily contact with the business of hip-hop and, happily, ended my long-ass E and F train rides into the city. I was back in Brooklyn, but to a very different 'hood than the one I'd grown up in. Until I moved to Fort G I'd been in the area only once before.

After picking up a girl at a disco on my eighteenth birthday, I took the subway back to Brooklyn with visions of horizontal enrichment dancing in my head. However, during the ride I noticed that she had healed cuts on both wrists. She told me that she'd attempted suicide twice. In addition, she revealed that she had a male roommate, and was in a quasi-romantic relationship. I just walked her to her door, kissed her on the cheek, and got lost trying to get home. I now realize that this woman lived just two blocks from my current address in Brooklyn, but in '85 Fort Greene was a foreign land.

I had no connection to the area. I had never had any friends who lived there. After that weird experience, I never dated any girls who lived there. All I knew was that Fort Greene was just east of downtown Brooklyn, where I had spent my whole childhood going shopping with my mother. When I did my internship at the *Phoenix* I actually worked just blocks from Fort Greene. Yet streets such as DeKalb, St. Felix, and Carlton were as foreign to me as avenues in Staten Island. I knew that the Fort Greene projects had produced the basketball greats Bernard and Albert King. The area was also always regarded as a hotbed for gang activity—first in the seventies, with the Tomahawks, and in the eighties, with the Decepticons.

Fort Greene, and my new place at 19 Willoughby Avenue, were easy to love. In contrast to where I'd grown up in Brownsville and lived in Queens, Fort Greene was very close to Manhattan. On almost every major subway line, Fort Greene was no more than two or three stops into Brooklyn, so going out, especially anywhere below Fourteenth Street, was made very convenient. The streets were lined with tall, thick trees fronting magnificent brownstones. There was a picturesque park with rolling hills and tennis courts, and in the fall it filled with hard, brown, fallen acorns that I used to collect and on occasion toss at friends. Fort Greene was close enough to Manhattan that I could leave my apartment at 7:30 P.M. and catch an 8:15 P.M. show at the Bottom Line in Greenwich Village, which made my life infinitely easier.

Plus, the apartment itself was a marvel. It was a duplex with wood floors, two bedrooms, twenty-foot-high ceilings, a large kitchen, exposed-brick walls, and a large backyard. I vowed when my family moved out of the projects that I would never live in a large apartment building again. However, I never imagined that I could live in a place this spacious.

I was able to afford this place because my quickie bio of Michael Jackson had been a bestseller. For the first time in my life I had disposable income, much of which I would squander on wine, women, and vinyl. But whatever I wasted in riches came back to me threefold in experience.

My first month in 19 Willoughby I actually slept upstairs in the long living room, in awe of all the space as I thought back to the bedroom and cramped closet I'd shared with my sister. I calculated that you could have fit our entire public housing apartment in my upstairs. I would live in 19 Willoughby from 1985 to 1992, the most important years of my life in terms of my immersion in music, film, writing, and sex. In 19 Willoughby I wrote five books, including my breakthrough work, *The Death of Rhythm and Blues*. I invested in *She's Gotta Have It*, and a couple of other movies, and wrote two produced screenplays. I fondly remember blasting Miles Davis's *Sketches of Spain* in that huge living room, having his muted trumpet fill the air as I made love with a girlfriend on the red carpet placed before the fireplace.

Having my own place, especially one with a working fireplace, was great for my sex life, but it wasn't what ultimately made me a bad boyfriend. It wasn't that I was unfaithful with other women. It was that now I was just in love with creativity. That's what truly turned me on and turned me out. At night I'd dream of sleeping in a bed filled up to my neck with my books. I saw myself as being warmed and comforted by my prose, the ink and paper sticking to my body like sweat. That was a passion with which no woman, no matter how sweet or sexy, could compete.

Alone in this large apartment my ambition grew, as if I had to think bigger to fill the space I was now living in. Sometimes it ate at me at night, forcing me out of bed, back to my legal pad to grind out one more record review, and to jot down ideas for books I was sure would change the world. It's likely I was overstimulated by all the vitality of that period's black culture. It was absolutely true that the talent around me was inspiring.

Going out to pick up take-out soul food at a basement spot on DeKalb, walking to the tasty Italian restaurant Cino's or to Junior's on Flatbush Avenue for thick chocolate cake, I'd stroll past the apartments of Spike Lee, writer Thulani Davis, a slew of jazz musicians (Lester Bowie, Wynton and Branford Marsalis, Cecil Taylor, Betty Carter), and other not as well known but vital writers, designers, musicians, and actors. The crackle of creative energy animated the air, as black folk made art all around me. It was a tactile, tangible feeling, and I adored it. With my take-out food in a bag I'd hurry back to 19 Willoughby to wolf down my meal and get back to work, anxious not to be left behind.

It's not that Fort Greene circa mideighties was paradise. One reason all these great brownstone apartments were affordable by young artists was crime. Just a long block from my apartment were several public housing projects, which bordered the park on the

Myrtle Avenue side. They weren't quite as grim as the Tilden projects I'd grown up in, but they were plenty tough. When crack began running amok in Brooklyn's streets, these projects were a center of trafficking, spawning a wave of dealers and addicts that had you keeping your eyes open at night.

My first week in 19 Willoughby I'd set up my office in the back bedroom, which had big gated windows looking into the backyard. I was sitting in front of my first laptop seeking inspiration when a man appeared in my backyard with a TV in his arms. He'd somehow hopped my neighbor's fence with it, and was preparing to do the same to mine to escape onto the street. I was about to call the cops when, over the fence abutting the street, two policemen hopped over and snagged the thief. I felt like I was watching a live theatrical version of the reality show *Cops*. Welcome to Fort Greene, I guess.

In all my years in Brooklyn I've never been mugged. There's only been one robbery at one of my places in Fort Greene, and it was my fault. As I was leaving one morning a FedEx package arrived. I got distracted as I was signing, and left my door open. When I got home my VCR was gone. Much worse, my satin *Soul Train* jacket, with my name embossed on the lapel, was stolen too. Somewhere out there is my personalized *Soul Train* jacket, a loss I mourn to this day.

The scene in Spike's 1992 film *Jungle Fever* in which Halle Berry's crackhead offers Wesley Snipes a blow job in front of his daughter was inspired by a real incident, when Branford Marsalis, in a kiddie park with his young son, was approached by a crack addict with a similarly repulsive offer. Branford subsequently left Fort Greene, as did many of my wave of black artists.

After *She's Gotta Have It* (which I'll get to in a bit) was released in 1986, Fort G became internationally known as home base to my generation of artists. What Spike's film did was expand that early community, and attract other artsy black folk. Chris Rock, Rosie Perez, rapper Daddy-O of Stetsasonic, Living Colour's Vernon Reid, actress Alva Rogers of *Daughters of the Dust*, saxophonist/bandleader Steve Coleman, and Def Jam executive Bill Stephney were among the wave that moved to Fort Greene post-Spike. The *New York Times* was among the many publications that profiled the area, making Fort Greene synonymous with a "Brooklyn boheme" vibe. Spike was very much the mayor of that moment, being the most celebrated artist, the biggest employer of local talent, and a buyer of real estate. At one point he owned five buildings in Fort Greene.

This mix of youth, creativity, and proximity meant parties were a regular staple of Fort Greene. I'd roll into the house of actor Wesley Snipes or cartoonist Barbara Brandon for food, drinks, and dancing. There are folks I saw at those parties who married each other, had kids and, in a few cases, are now divorced. There was lots of sex to be had, and lots of cheating too.

One tangible document of the creative ferment in Fort Greene, and the overall New York black community, was a photo taken by Anthony Barboza for an unpublished *New York Times Magazine* piece on the "new black aesthetic" by Trey Ellis in 1989. It was taken at the then new offices of Spike's 40 Acres and a Mule Filmworks on DeKalb Avenue across from Brooklyn Technical High School. Most in the photo were residents of brownstone Brooklyn—Spike; the writer Lisa Jones; her sister, the art historian Keli; visual artist Lorna Simpson; guitarist Vernon Reid; Bill Stephney; Chris Rock; and myself. In addition, there were fellow travelers from Harlem,

Warrington and Reggie Hudlin, and downtown Manhattan icons like theater director George C. Wolf, Fab Five Freddie, and Russell Simmons.

While living at 19 Willoughby I learned what kind of writer, what kind of lover, and even what kind of son I was. But the most surprising revelation was that I was a mentor and, like my mother, a kind of teacher. Not only did I write about artists and hang with them, but I found myself being a kind of one-man support network for people—mostly aspiring artists—I believed in. During the mid-eighties they tended to be my peers, gifted folks who needed some contacts or an introduction to someone to move forward. This dynamic was at work with Russell, as well as with Andre Harrell, a so-so MC who'd go on to form the signature rap label Uptown, and the indie filmmaking brothers Warrington and Reggie Hudlin in the years before they broke through with the hit comedy *House Party*.

Over time I grew more settled in the role, and I became a more hands-on mentor, either collaborating with younger artists or critiquing screenplays, essays, or recordings with tough love. My attorney used to tell me I was a natural producer, but at first I wasn't sure if that was a good thing. Producers in film and television seemed more businessmen than artists, and I always saw myself as a creator.

Yet, as I came to understand the place where mentoring, criticism, and producing overlapped, I moved into that sphere more gracefully than I'd ever imagined. Somewhere in my makeup—perhaps from my mother—I had a nurturing gene that first manifested itself at 19 Willoughby, and that would blossom in the years ahead, and would, in fact, define my life, and self-image, as much as writing.

A few of the people I helped became household names, but, like the majority of ambitious folks who use the city as a springboard, most either went on to humble careers or didn't make it at all. Sometimes they were too insecure to survive the disappointments and rejection. Others allowed their egos to blind them to their limitations, and sometimes, despite immense talent, never learned to play well with others. Whether these artists won or lost, I found being close to their struggles exciting and drew lessons from them that I applied to myself.

The most important lesson was to measure myself not by sudden success or rapid failure but by my body of work. My dream was to write a bookshelf of volumes, so many that one day I might drown in them, paper and ink suffocating me in an ocean of my own thoughts. More practically, I wanted to have a full, active life, and being productive seemed the way to ensure that.

Many writers aspire to be Ralph Ellison, to write a starburst of a book that would light the literary sky forever. I was more interested in emulating Richard Wright, Langston Hughes, or Gordon Parks, all of whom had long, varied careers that produced many works and embraced many disciplines. This philosophy gave me patience and a perspective on success (or lack of it). So many folks I met burned out on early success and early failure. If you were in it for the long haul, rolling with the highs and lows was easier, knowing it was all part of a larger whole. Jimi Hendrix may be a deeply romantic figure in our culture, but I'd rather have the body of work of Prince and Stevie Wonder (not to mention the life span).

Achieving sustained excellence is what I preached to others and sought for myself.

One of my favorite stories from that period in the eighties revolves around Prince and, partially, 19 Willoughby. I'd been an early fan of Prince Rogers Nelson, seeing him with a group of college pals at the Bottom Line in fall 1980, just before the release of *Dirty Mind*. I did my first interview for *Record World* with him in January '81, and wrote about him a lot in *Billboard* throughout the 1980s, developing a relationship of sorts with him and people in his camp.

One day at *Billboard* I got a call from his road manager, Alan Leeds. Prince wanted to give me a personal preview of his *Parade* album. I felt as though being an early advocate was paying off. Not only was I flattered, but I was hopeful that I could weasel an exclusive interview out of him, so I sat at my desk at 19 Willoughby on that Saturday as instructed.

A couple of hours went by, and I was beginning to feel a little foolish, when the phone finally rang. A young woman's voice, quite childlike and breathy, told me to come to an address near the United Nations. On the subway ride into Manhattan I scribbled down possible questions, and made sure my tape recorder was working. At a doorman building just a block or so from the UN I was directed to an elevator that ascended to the penthouse. The door slid open, and a fluffy white poodle strolled in and inspected me.

As I stepped into the living room, Prince was nowhere to be seen, but my disappointment was short-lived, as a tall, platinum blonde with big eyes and red lips came toward me. The tall, big-boned woman in the tight black dress and white pumps was Jill Jones. Prince fans will remember her for her small role as a waitress in *Purple Rain,* for taking off her panties in the middle of the street in the only highlight of the horrid *Graffiti Bridge,* and for a late-eighties solo album filled with recycled Vanity 6 riffs.

On this afternoon, however, Jill was my gracious host at what was clearly Prince's New York pad. The living room was dominated by a white piano located strategically under a large round skylight. The remnants of dead candles were scattered atop it. Next to the piano was a sofa buried beneath a mountain of purple-and-gold-leafed pillows. I sat in a white cushioned armchair facing a component set that featured a reel-to-reel tape player. As Jill brought over red wine and cheese, I heard *Parade* for the first time.

This may have seemed very cozy. Yet the whole time I sat listening I had this weird feeling I was being watched. Whether he was stashed in the darkened back rooms to my right, or had small cameras or mikes hidden around the room, I felt his presence. I knew Jill would report back how I reacted to the music (and to her), but I figured he'd have some more hi-tech tools. He was Prince, after all.

My listening session over, I chatted a bit with the adorable Ms. Jones. She was in New York studying acting and taking voice lessons and tending to her puppy. The silly part of me wanted to invite her out to dinner. The smart part of me headed back to Brooklyn. My next *Billboard* column was about my private listening session, which meant Prince had gotten what he wanted—great press without having to answer a single question.

I saw August Wilson's *Ma Rainey's Black Bottom* in 1984 on Broadway, and would go to see every one of his ten plays, and not just on Broadway, but in New Haven; Boston; Washington, D.C.; and Los Angeles. Like a Grateful Dead–head I traveled around America, watching how Wilson rewrote his plays, finding inspiration in the work of my great literary obsession.

On opening night of *Joe Turner's Come and Gone,* March 26, 1988, I sat in the front row in the right aisle seat. Wilson's drama of a haunted man and his daughter, searching for their lost wife and mother in Pittsburgh circa 1911, was rich with African mysticism and the burdens racism imposed on its former slaves. In *Turner's* climatic moment Harold Loomis and Martha Pentecost, played by two then unknown thespians, Delroy Lindo and Angela Bassett, struggle with the past, God, and a knife.

When the lights came up, Bassett stood before me onstage, the stage lights twinkling off her eyes and reflecting off those now legendary cheekbones. Between the play's end and the after-party at Sardi's, my date headed home—she'd just gotten in from a convention, and was worn out by Wilson's epic play—while I headed in.

I found Wilson on the second floor leaning against a wall, smoking a handy supply of cigarettes. Extremely fair skinned, with a thick salt and pepper beard, Wilson had a big, bearish demeanor, friendly and distant at the same time. Ms. Bassett was more accessible. I gushed about how good she was, how attractive I found her, and anything else I could try in an ultimately successful effort to get her phone number. It was the start of a sweet friendship.

I ended up riding back to Fort Greene with Spike, who'd also been at the party, and commenting enthusiastically about Delroy Lindo and Angela. (A few years later both would play key roles in *Malcolm X* and Lindo would eventually play Spike's father in *Crook-*

lyn.) Being toyed with by Prince, and meeting August Wilson and Angie Bassett at the beginnings of their careers, are just a few of the snapshots from that explosion of eighties black pop culture. I'm not sure if that period will have the historic resonance of the Harlem Renaissance of the twenties or the Black Arts movement of the sixties, but that generation, post-soul and mostly pre-hip-hop, both capitalized on existing opportunities and created new models for success.

TALKING HEAD

Looking back, I can see that my career, and that of my eighties peers, was aided to a great degree by a profound change in white America's attitudes toward black creativity. Despite the outright hostility of the ruling GOP administration toward the poor and people of color, the mass public had no problem embracing Whitney Houston, Bill Cosby, Eddie Murphy, Toni Morrison, Wynton Marsalis, and a long list of superb black talent spread over a wide range of disciplines.

Being in New York, with access to several publications with a national profile, I found myself writing at a time of great talent, unprecedented success, and a grudging acknowledgment that black people could actually explain black creative expressions better than white folks could. Well, maybe I exaggerate a bit. At least they began putting us on an equal playing field (though papers and mags like the *New York Times* or *Rolling Stone* rarely employed black critics). But overall a space opened up where I and many others could build a national profile via white media, which, in turn, led to book contracts, speaking engagements, and teaching gigs. The mainstream acceptance of black creativity had a trickle-down effect on myself and many others.

I think my first national television appearance was on CBS's

Morning Show in 1984 or so, when I joined a panel talking about the major summer tours. I must have done all right, because I soon became a regular talking head on news broadcasts and music-related documentaries, a great many of which were done for British TV. It amazed me that I kept getting asked to do on-camera interviews, since I knew I had a tendency to mumble when excited, and my fashion sense has always been questionable.

Every time a request came in it made me think of watching ABC's *Wide World of Sports* with my mother. The weekly Saturday afternoon broadcast was legendary for its great opening voice-over, promising "The thrill of victory and the agony of defeat," and being broadcaster Howard Cosell's platform to media stardom. Fights were regular features of the broadcast, and we'd often watch the ever-increasing number of black fighters dispatch the ever-decreasing number of great white hopes.

Actually more dangerous for the race than the boxing contests were the postfight interviews. Ma would sit with me and hope that the black boxers "could talk." Nothing upset her more than a black man on TV who couldn't pronounce vowels, didn't use Gs, or otherwise viewed standard English as a third language. She'd watch ABC's loquacious Cosell ask them questions with her psychic fingers crossed. Ma liked the hard-charging style of Joe Frazier, the relentless Philadelphia fighter who was Muhammad Ali's greatest rival, but squirmed whenever Smokin' Joe got near a microphone.

With this as a backdrop you can imagine Cassius Clay/Muhammad Ali was a welcome presence on our black-and-white. Ma was especially taken with the post–Nation of Islam boxer, a man who spoke slower, more purposefully, and with more heart than bluster.

His youthful bravado was still in evidence, but it was tempered by a maturity that made him an international hero and, subsequently, an American one.

At no point in those days did my mother and I ever entertain the idea that I'd be doing television interviews, talking about sports, movies, or music. Unless you were a fighter or a civil rights leader, you weren't talking on TV in the sixties. Black experts on anything but "the movement" and the "Negro problem" were rare, unless you threw a jab or a baseball.

So when these on-camera opportunities started coming my way, I never wanted any black folks flinching when my face popped up. I never wanted to be known for leaving off Gs, mispronouncing (or misusing) big words, or stumbling in my articulation, or to do anything to make my mother cringe. I never aspired to being a TV talk-show host or correspondent, but it quickly became clear that being an "expert" raised the profile of my work and helped sell books.

A turning point in my talking head career came via an appearance in 1986 on the *Today* show to promote *Where Did Our Love Go?*. Getting a spot on the NBC franchise was a coup. Even better, I was to be interviewed by Bryant Gumbel, who'd made the big jump from handling the NFL Sunday pregame show, bringing his crisp delivery and smart professionalism to early-morning television. Gumbel didn't kiss up to guests—he asked tough questions—and did not suffer fools. As a young journalist, I respected him immensely, since, in his own way, he was a revolutionary figure. Gumbel presented himself as he was. He didn't curry favor with a toothy smile or toss in slang or otherwise play the race card to cozy up to viewers. He reveled in his competence, a character trait that could tip over into arrogance. I always thought that if one of Sidney Poitier's characters from the sixties survived into the eighties, he'd have been as composed and cocky as Gumbel was on the *Today* show.

In the greenroom that morning I sat watching a monitor and had tea, amazed at being in the famous building at 30 Rockefeller Plaza, about to be interviewed on national TV about my first work of serious nonfiction. I'd done a lot of TV in the wake of writing that quickie bio of Michael Jackson in 1984, but the Motown book and the *Today* show was the big time. I had a sense that I'd arrived as a writer. I wasn't worried that Bryant was wearing out some actress with withering sarcasm. She didn't seem too smart, and as I said, he didn't kiss up to even ingenues. I was just convinced he'd give me love.

Walking into the chilly studio, knowing that I'd have four minutes on national television to describe my book, was a heady feeling. I was so gassed that I didn't take it as a bad sign that Bryant shook my hand stiffly, made no small talk, and looked down at his notes during the entire commercial break. He was a pro's pro. No need for him to chat me up. Save the good cheer for on air.

Red light comes on. Clips of Motown artists are screened. He reads off a teleprompter. I hope my cheap blue suit looks presentable under NBC's unforgiving lights. He starts in with that clipped, energetic delivery. And his tone is as cool and probing as a urologist's hand. He's not treating me as a "brother" but as a subject, one who has written a slightly controversial, often critical volume about the greatest black business of the twentieth century. He asks me why I didn't speak to Gordy (he wouldn't grant me an interview), about my sources (the juiciest stuff came from the in-house band members, now known as the Funk Brothers), and, finally, he wonders accusingly about my depiction of Gordy himself.

Of course, it was clear by then that Gumbel was holding me up to the same standard he'd hold up any other historian. Show and prove, young man. Let me see if your work is as intellectually rigorous as it needs to be. Because of the high-profile venue and the aggressive questioning, this is absolutely the toughest interview I'd ever (would ever) experience. Being young and more naïve than I would have admitted, I resented Gumbel's interrogation. I came through all right. In fact, I even got a little flip with him, which just came out as me defending myself.

But, afterward, as I wrote other books, I realized that Bryant Gumbel had done me a tremendous favor. Prior to the *Today* show I had thought that because I was black, Bryant would toss me softball questions. He cured me of that expectation forever. No matter who came to interview me or what subject I was speaking about, I had to be prepared for anything. I had to know what I wanted to say, how I wanted to say it, and, perhaps most important, how to handle the questions I didn't care for. I'd been a good interview before that, but from then on I worked hard on perfecting the art of the sound bite.

The truth is, Gumbel was an anomaly. I'd find that most television interviewers were not nearly that tough or tenacious. In fact, on live TV, the interviewee has a lot of control, since there's a limited amount of time for follow-up questions. You can use phrases like "That's a very good point, but what's really important" to lead the conversation in another direction. I figured out that in the hierarchy of interviewers, those on TV tended to be the least well prepared and most passive, so you can manipulate the interview more easily (compared to doing print and radio).

The bookend to this story is that, a decade later, I was working as a producer on Chris Rock's HBO show, supervising interviews. We booked Bryant Gumbel, and I did the preinterview with him, and prepared questions with Chris. By this time Gumbel was nearing the end of his increasingly contentious tenure at the *Today* show. In fact, he was grappling with bad press about his failing marriage and his rocky relationships with his coworkers. It was weird to be interviewing the man who had, inadvertently, schooled me in the art of TV presentation. Even funnier was that we were preparing to do the type of interview I'd hoped for years earlier—softball questions that, in this case, would be spiked with setups for Rock to be funny. Life is filled with funny little ironies, and one of them is that most of your best lessons are taught outside the classroom.

VOICES INSIDE MY HEAD

Where Did Our Love Go? The Rise and Fall of the Motown Sound had been an emotional journey and challenge for me, both wrapping up a childhood obsession and establishing me as a serious writer. But there was a conceptual leap I wished to make, and it was daunting. I had a title for a book in my head, *The Death of Rhythm and Blues*. It was an idea that went back to those mornings listening to Eddie O'Jay's *Soul at Sunrise* on LIB. I wanted to look back not only at the how black music had changed, but at how the institutions that supported it (radio stations, mom-and-pop record retailers, concert venues and clubs, record labels) had evolved as well.

Two ideas would animate the project: SOLAR Records honcho Dick Griffey (later Suge Knight's mentor) used to say that as oil was to the Arabs, our music was to us, a lucrative and seemingly endless economic resource; and two, the music reflected where African Americans were in our historical evolution in American society. Ultimately I would revisit the journey from segregation to integration via popular music, looking specifically at what had been lost and gained in this process. Great idea, huh? I just had to figure out how to write it.

Over my years at *Billboard* I had accumulated scores of interviews. Moreover, the pack rat in me had all the material I'd used to write *The Michael Jackson Story* and the Motown book in file cabinets, plus lots of articles and memorabilia I'd been saving for a more in-depth inquiry. Now I had to interview folks with tighter, more focused questions. I began acquiring tons of juicy individual stories that personalized this larger tale. I looked at Louis Jordan's post–World War II crossover success, the colorful promotion men who traversed the nation as musical traveling salesmen of soul, and on to hip-hop's place as a revival of black music's vitality.

But writing a book isn't journalism. It takes a larger vision, tons of thought, and a grasp of narrative. So I got lost in the devilish details, and lost the thread of my story. In one disastrous draft I even had a fictional DJ character, who represented the spirit of black music throughout the twentieth century. This was an absolutely horrible idea that I had made worse by executing it badly.

In early 1987, which ironically—and maybe not coincidentally—was a pivotal year in hip-hop's artistic development (Public Enemy, LL Cool J, Boogie Down Productions, Big Daddy Kane, Rakim), I found my keys to unlocking the history of R&B. I'd befriended the producer-songwriter Mtume at the start of my career. Aside from creating huge hits for Stephanie Mills, Phyllis Hyman, and his self-titled band, this ex–Miles Davis percussionist had, as a young man, been caught up in the maelstrom of radical politics. He had been down with Ron Karenga's US Movement in Los Angeles and, later, part of the nationalist community that rose to prominence in Newark after the brutal late-sixties riots.

Because of his understanding of black music and politics, Mtume was an ideal person to bounce ideas off of on the phone, as I paced my big living room at 19 Willoughy. Equally important, Mtume introduced me to Harold Cruse's *The Crisis of the Negro Intellectual*, a blazingly brilliant analysis of the challenges, and compromises, that bedeviled the best and the brightest of our race. Cruse's book became the template for *The Death of Rhythm and Blues*, its structure showing me how to mold my own argument. It was setting the bar high to even try to follow Cruse's lead, but the only way to be even slightly good is to aspire to greatness.

The other crucial bit of info that helped me came at a black music conference in, I believe, Atlanta. Two of the music's great old promotion men, Joe Medlin and Dave Clark, men with careers that dated back to the Depression, sat me down in the hotel lobby one afternoon and schooled me on the existence of the "Harvard Report." Joe, a large film noir character, was an intimidating man who loved fedoras and cigars, and had a voice as raw as sandpaper, and Dave, a wiry dandy who at sixty was rocking leather pants and Bally loafers, and would one day marry a woman thirty years his junior, told me about a notorious report CBS Records had commissioned around 1970 on how to penetrate the black music market.

Sounded like the tangible example I needed to illustrate my overall argument about how the culture had been altered in the seventies. Problem was, neither man had a copy. Like clockwork Joyce McCrae, a white woman who'd worked for years with Jackie Wilson, and who'd been an intimate of the Jackson family, sat down. Somewhere in her house she had a copy. After lots of follow-up phone calls, I received a photocopied version of the report in the mail, and immediately, it became my book's Rosetta Stone. Completed at the dawn of the seventies, the "Harvard Report" was a very detailed plan for how a major corporate-financed record company could invest in new labels, recruit black executive talent, and increase its overall market share via R&B/soul artists.

Though it was written some fifteen years before I acquired it, I recognized its DNA in the actions of CBS, Warner Bros., RCA, and every other major label. In retrospect, the "Harvard Report" was more a commonsense business strategy than a plan to re-create black culture. Still, its existence gave my narrative a clear demarcation line, a before-and-after snapshot of the R&B world. As happened so often during my years as a music journalist, listening to the wise old men of R&B showed me a path forward.

Inside 19 Willoughby, I grinded on that book, giving myself a goal of writing seven pages a night no matter how long it took. Quincy Jones had told me a few years earlier about "ass power" and now it was my turn to flex. With the aid of my editors, *The Death of Rhythm and Blues* grew coherent.

On its release in 1988, *The Death of Rhythm and Blues* received prominent reviews in the *New York Times*, the *Boston Globe*, and other major publications. I won some awards, and was nominated for others. Most important, it was a project that made the leap from bold idea to well-argued book, from critical formulation to a real work of history. The creative struggles of the early writing taught me valuable lessons, the most important of which was the necessity of a strong theme, an animating idea that drives the narrative, informing everything, from title to chapter, even to digressions. To me, theme—whether it's a novel, screenplay, or nonfiction narrative—determines what gets left in and what gets taken out. It's not an exact science, of course, but once you have that theme, it's so much easier to separate the forest from the trees.

I also now understood that artistic failure was an essential and educational aspect of doing great work. In a culture that craves quick results, mistakes, bad decisions, and awkward execution are paths to clarity. So many people get frustrated and stop working when confronted by failed attempts at art. You have to forgive yourself for the mess you made and, like a child, pick up your blocks and stack them up again. If you can ultimately understand why you went wrong, the correct path will reveal itself. Self-criticism in the middle of creating something can be an artistic dead end. You've got to stay open to accidents and to your subconscious, 'cause it'll tell you what you need to know.

And after the agony comes the fun. I had an amazing party for that book in the summer of '88. It was a humid summer afternoon, and all my windows were open in search of an elusive breeze, as the upstairs and then the backyard filled with friends from many worlds. The late Jack "the Rapper" Gibson, a legendary black radio personality, was profiled in the book, and he flew up from Atlanta. Debra Crable, the doe-eyed, gorgeous host of the syndicated *Ebony Jet Showcase*, rolled in from Chicago. Model Veronica Webb and a bevy of beauties came through. So did Broadway diva Melba Moore, and my pal Russell Simmons, who complained all day about the cracks in Brooklyn's sidewalks, and wondered why I still lived in the ghetto.

Those are just the names I remember off the top of my head. My memory was overwhelmed by the variety of folks who ate and drank in my backyard and living room, and on my front steps. At one point I went outside and found Russell and Melba Moore on my stoop talking, a more unlikely duo it's hard to imagine. When my mother, my sister, and my then eight-year-old niece, Ebony, arrived, the circle was complete. It wasn't a dance party like Ma's

Saturday night throw-downs, but it was as close as I'll ever come. It took me weeks to get the toilet working right again after the heavy use. The energy of all those amazing people in my space lingered in 19 Willoughby for months afterward. I've always felt that there was something magical about that gathering that propelled *The Death of Rhythm and Blues* into the world, and has given it a long, successful life.

▭▭

Fort Greene Park was just down the block from me, so I was still running a bit to stay fit and centered. I'd tackle those steps that you see at the end of *She's Gotta Have It*, and then run up and down the hills by the tennis courts. But most of my searches for transcendence during this period of my life were behind my primitive PC and at my stereo. For the first time in my life I had a place all to myself. Aside from listening to music professionally, to write reviews or prepare for interviews, I could play particular songs as often as I wanted, a dream come true for a kid who'd lived with family and roommates my whole life. I'd play certain records seven, eight, or nine times in a row, getting lost in them with no intention of finding my way home. CDs were just coming on the market, so most of the time it was me moving the needle back on a 45 or 12-inch single, or carefully landing on the right groove on an album.

Certain records still send me on a reverie: Aretha Franklin's "Call Me"; Led Zep's "Trampled Underfoot"; Womack & Womack's "Baby, I'm Scared of You"; Miles's *Sketches of Spain*; LL Cool J's "Jack the Ripper." And, perhaps most of all, anything sung by Anita Baker, starting with her first hit, "Angel." These days Anita's no longer in fashion. Two generations of soul sirens have come and gone since she first appeared. Plus, she took a long hiatus in the nineties to raise kids, which has diluted her appeal, but for me she once conjured dreamscapes like no other vocalist.

The first time I heard her voice I was lying on a friend's sofa bed in Los Angeles. KJLH, a once great hit-making R&B station, played "Angel," and I was entranced. The tune was laid-back, with jazzy chords and a hook that was more spoken than sung by Ms. Baker. Her voice was throaty and womanly, though Baker could invoke a girlish naïveté when a song required it. Her voice harkened back to the bluesy past of black pop music, yet was also well suited to the cognac aesthetic of the day.

I found out that Baker recorded for an upstart R&B indie label named Beverly Glen. Though short-lived, Beverly Glen released two gems in the middle of the soulfully deprived eighties—Baker's debut album, *The Songstress*, and Bobby Womack's amazing comeback recording, *The Poet*. While "Angel" put Baker on the map, it wasn't until her Elektra records debut, *Rapture*, in 1986 that she exploded, and I was really able to turn my enthusiasm for her into articles. I wrote a lead review about Baker for the *Village Voice*, and quite a bit about her in the pages of *Billboard*. I even coined a phrase, "retro nuevo," to describe the blend of old and new I felt her work represented.

When Baker made her New York concert debut at Avery Fisher Hall on the heels of *Rapture*, I was in the fourth row. That night she certainly fulfilled my need for the transcendental. Many in the crowd must have shared my eagerness to hear her, because Baker was rewarded with standing ovations after her third song, seventh song, and tenth song. Somewhere buried in my archives are my notes on that show. I don't remember what songs inspired that response, but I do know I've never attended a show for what was, in essence, a debuting singer where the audience was so passionately in love. On that particular night Baker and the audience were in absolute sync. It was on that night two decades ago that I decided that, if I ever got married (something still in doubt all these years later), Baker (or a recording of her) singing "Angel" or "Sweet Love" would be played as my bride and I walked down the aisle.

I remembered thinking as I left Avery Fisher Hall that it was nights like this that made all the bad gigs, the uninspired professionalism, and formulaic performances I endured worth it. It was why I waded through the piles of vinyl that surrounded my desk at *Billboard*. I was always looking for that music and performer who, however briefly, touched the divine and shared that feeling with me. During my prime years as a music critic there were others who did it for me (Tracy Chapman, Babyface, Bruce Springsteen, Luther Vandross, Fela, Aretha, Paul Simon, John Coltrane, and Miles), but something about Anita Baker made me feel it so profoundly.

Looking back to my late twenties, I think now that I was seeking something in art that was lacking in my life. While I gloried in these transporting musical moments, I couldn't connect emotionally with people in an equally satisfying way. I was in love at least twice during these years, and had strong romantic connections to a series of amazing girlfriends. But I never married, and rarely totally committed. I can chalk some of that up to just being a horny young man. I think that's understandable.

However, I know there was more to it. This feeling I'd had when I was a teenager, of being outside of my own emotions, and of being dispassionate about my life, affected my love affairs. I could feel a cold, distant part of myself take over. That part of me could find fault with my love for any woman. It wasn't that I attacked them, but I criticized myself out of the relationship. I wasn't listening enough. I wasn't sympathetic enough. I was too busy. I was married to my writing.

Whatever I said to them (and told myself), it was just a justification for not truly committing. It felt like something inside was blocking me, and I cried about this inability quite a bit during this period. I'd play Otis Redding and John Coltrane alone in my high-ceilinged living room, drowning in my melancholy for several spins of the record, and then I'd vow to do better and be more open the next time. It was sad and funny that I could be so damn emotional about a record, but not about the women who loved me.

EAST NEW YORK

While my life in Fort Greene (and beyond) was filled with the upwardly mobile ambience of art, romance, and parties, I was still deeply connected to the tougher Brooklyn of my youth, a world just a subway ride away. Mideighties New York was suffering through the height of crackmania, and all the family I cared about lived in the urban war zone known as East New York.

Back when I was in college my mother had put together enough money to buy a house, which was actually on the same street as our Fairfield Towers apartment. She'd bought a two-story home at 812 New Jersey Avenue, about four blocks from 1081 New Jersey, and just below Linden Boulevard, one of Brooklyn's main thoroughfares, the one that ran through the heart of East New York.

At some point during my college years the Fairfield Towers housing complex had reached its tipping point, and all my white friends, and quite a few of my middle-class black ones, had already split or were in the process of fleeing. Ma's decision to buy a house had many ramifications, none bigger than its effect on her love affair with Stan. She had invested herself in the relationship, half joking to me that she'd "made him a man" by pushing him to pursue an assistant principal's job. For his part, Stan had stayed in a monogamous relationship with a woman with two kids, not something every single guy would do. Over time it became clear that Stan's relatives, particularly his mother, were strongly against him inheriting a ready-made family.

Ma's desire to own a home made Stan face a tough decision: Would he buy a house with her, or not? Would he be with Arizona George for the long run? Together their teachers' salaries would have gotten them a bigger house in a better neighborhood. Stan procrastinated. Ma waited. He couldn't make up his mind. Ma viewed his hesitation as a negative comment on his commitment to her. So, being a stubborn little woman, she just went on and bought her own damn house. That bold move effectively ended their relationship. They saw each other for a while after we moved into 812, but the bond that had sustained them for years had been irreparably broken.

Over the years I'd spot Stan at sporting events—once he even called out to me—but the man had broken my mother's heart, so there was no place for him in mine. However, he did leave a small mark on our future. As a housewarming present, Stan gave Ma a black calico cat that Andrea named Baby. To this day either my mother or sister has always kept a cat as a pet, a lingering bit of Stan in their lives. Ma tried to hide her disappointment from Andrea and me, but I knew it hurt her deeply. I don't think she's ever loved another man since.

As a result of all this, 812 New Jersey was always a melancholy residence. We had a basement with a washer/dryer, a concrete backyard, two bathrooms, and an upstairs storage room, the kind of space we'd never had before. Maybe because my room was smaller than at 1081, maybe because of how and why Ma purchased it, that house never seemed that happy to me.

Not helping my feelings about 812 was that there was no escaping the fact that by moving below Linden, we were now officially back in a ghetto. Unlike Brownsville, which was dominated by acres of public housing, East New York had block upon block of attached two-story homes. Not row houses, since they didn't share the same architectural style, but all the ones around us had little ledges that could allow the adventurous to walk from one end of the block to the other. Our integrated life in Fairfield had already disappeared, so moving back into a 100 percent black environment was no big deal. Plus, we were on a block of homeowners, so it wasn't like we'd moved back into the projects.

But, like most of New York's working-class 'hoods in the late seventies, the quality of life in East New York was declining rapidly. While owning a home was an economic step up for Ma and us, everything else around us went to hell. The night of the infamous 1977 blackout the last shopping strips in the area were robbed clean of appliances and furniture. Our neighbors hauled them home on their backs or tag-teamed carrying them. The stores that were ravaged then didn't come back. Whatever short-term gains people made the night of the blackout were fleeting. When the morning came, and order was restored, we saw that the economic backbone of East New York was broken and, all these years later, it is yet to be fully repaired.

Our new neighbors were an eclectic group of working-class people. There was a pious family of Jehovah's Witnesses. There was a tough family of Caribbean immigrants. There were our next-door neighbors, the Griffiths, a family of rowdy boys, most of whom would join the Five Percent nation and be renamed True God and Powerful. Across the street from our house was an elementary school where, in the summer, mobile DJs would blast Kraftwerk's "Trans-Europe Express" and MFSB's "Love Is the Message" for hours on end, giving me inklings of the transition in New York street music from disco to hip-hop.

After I moved out, first to Queens and then to Fort Greene, the area became drenched in drugs and its attendant violence. I got into the habit of listening to CBS News Radio 88 before I went to sleep. Late at night I'd go into my bedroom after writing and listen to the overnight news. So many times there were stories of drug-related drive-bys or suspicious fires that had happened in East New York. I'd listen tensely, always worried that an incident at 812 New Jersey Avenue would end up on the police blotter.

This wasn't idle anxiety. My sister had made several bad choices that made my fear well founded. Starting in high school, and then through a sad short-lived college career, Andrea had grown more rebellious. Whereas once she had been a straight A student, school fell by the wayside for her as she concentrated her energies in the street. Soon it became clear that drugs were becoming increasingly central to her life. Andrea, always an aggressive soul, became even more short-tempered and volatile. My mother and sister became engaged in a hot war, not just over Andrea's state of mind, but over the future of Ebony, my sister's first child. While Ebony was being raised by Andrea, she was still living under her grandmother's roof. So the arguments in 812 weren't just over my sister's behavior, but over how to raise a little girl.

I always sided with my mother in these battles, but Andrea didn't really care what I thought about her. She was going to do what she wanted how she wanted. During my years at 19 Willoughby our communications became brief and, at best, cordial. Sometimes she'd try to get me to see her side of things. "Ma is getting in my business," she'd argue, as though her mother was suppose to ignore her daughter's decay. These arguments made me incredibly angry at her, forcing us even further apart. I felt like she was trying to manipulate me, that every conversation had a purpose and that she was never being honest with me.

Things would get worse. As East New York was ravaged by crack, any family that could escape did. A home on New Jersey Avenue on the end of the block nearest Linden Boulevard became abandoned. About a month or so later some people removed the "For Sale" sign and moved in. They weren't a family, though. They were squatters. Even worse, they were drug dealers. These were lean and hungry young men who ran wires into neighboring backyards to steal electricity, and they began having noisy visitors day and night. Most folks on the block were rightfully freaked out by their appearance.

Not Andrea. My sister befriended this posse and began spending increasing amounts of time at their squat. Her relationship with one posse member escalated into a brief marriage and the birth of her second daughter, Leigh. Saddled with two young daughters and complicated relationships with both fathers, Andrea became increasingly angry. I felt very distant from my sister, viewing her now as the destructive force in our family, and I was constantly having to choose between my mother and my sister, which is a terrible position to be put in. Visiting 812 New Jersey became a chore, since I was confident I'd always end up in the middle of a nasty argument between the two women I loved most in the world. Whenever I spent time with my nieces I found myself in an untenable place—being very affectionate and loving with them while withholding any emotion I felt for Andrea except frustration.

I urged Ma to toss Andrea out or move herself. Even if it meant pushing Ebony out with her, I worried that my mother was being put in grave danger by Andrea's presence in the house. I could argue until I was blue in the face, but Ma felt she could not abandon Ebony. And even though she wouldn't admit it, she couldn't let Andrea go. As long as Andrea was nearby, she could, perhaps, save her from the streets.

By supporting my mother, I became my sister's de facto enemy. It was such a weird journey my family had taken. We'd gone from being a tight team working to escape the projects to a dysfunctional family in a two-story home. The chaos of Brooklyn's streets, which we'd barely avoided for years, now controlled our lives.

Few people in Fort Greene, or any of my other worlds, knew how complicated my family situation had become. All they knew was that I was writing books, yapping on the tube, and involved with high-profile types. Despite all that activity, I was scared for those I loved, yet determined not to let the druggy undertow pull me under. My mother urged me to keep on pushing with my work, to achieve, and to make her proud. I guess I felt like my life was a validation of her life, quelling any doubts that she might have had about how she had raised Andrea and me. And so I did that. I pushed and pushed, and I still do.

SPIKE

I first became aware of Spike Lee via public television. Sometime around 1983 I saw a broadcast of *Joe's Bed-Stuy Barbershop* on New York's channel 13, and I was electrified by the shock of recognition. This depiction of a barbershop owner deep in debt to a suave philosophy-spouting loan shark was the first film I'd ever seen that resembled the Brooklyn I knew—not simply the gorgeously photographed streets and buildings, but the bits of slang, body language, and relaxed black flavor that oozed out of every frame. Even if I hadn't been aware that this student Academy Award–winning film had been directed by a homeboy, I would have known this film had to have been molded by black hands.

Turned out that Spike and I had a mutual friend, an aspiring filmmaker, who arranged for us to meet at a Chinese restaurant on Seventh Avenue in Midtown. Spike had on a boxy red tam, gold wire-framed glasses, a small, bemused face. Don't remember much about the conversation other than that Spike really wanted to do music videos. I hooked him up with some executives, though no gigs came from these biz introductions (a quite embarrassing fact for these same executives, who'd later try to win rights to Spike's soundtracks).

I kept in loose contact with Spike over the next year or so. I remember meeting with him about a movie idea I had called *Empire,* a Motown roman à clef that never went past the treatment stage. As I said, in early 1985 I was still living in Queens and about to move to Fort Greene, when I (literally) received a wake-up call from Spike, and we reconnected.

At the time of my move I was knee-deep in the music business. Hanging with Spike reawakened two old passions. One was attending basketball games. From my childhood into my college years I had attended a lot of games at the Garden, mostly the Knicks, but also my alma mater, St. John's University. But as a young adult, my *Billboard* gig had filled my nights with concerts, nightclubs, and industry soirees.

To my amazement, Spike, who was working at an independent film distributor in the Village, and lived in a cramped two-room hovel, actually had Knicks season tickets. Years before he became the city's most identifiable Knicks fan, Spike was dropping several Gs to see a squad going down in flames due to a knee injury to star (and Fort Greene native) Bernard King. His seats were in nosebleed territory, up in section 308, just ten rows from the cheapest seats in the 400s; their saving grace was that they were situated at midcourt, so you had a panoramic, albeit distant, view of the court.

Before every game Spike would stop at a candy shop in front of MSG, get a mint milk shake, and then sit celebrating brief moments of Knicks competence, but more often cursing the ineptitude of referees and coaches. The passion for the game that would make him an (in)famous fan was already much in evidence.

The year the Knicks won the draft rights to Georgetown's Patrick Ewing, number one in the NBA draft, I bought my own season tickets. I managed to sit in the same section as Spike, about two rows behind him. For the next twenty years, through lousy teams and two runs to the NBA Finals, I held on to those tickets. Like Spike I'd move from my original seats, though obviously never as close to the court as my friend. Still, because of his example, the Knicks became one of the most enduring financial commitments of my life.

Spike, as everyone now knows, is an intense sports fan. Yet in all the years I've known him, I've never seen Spike hoist a jumper, toss a football, or swing a bat. Guys who grew up with him in Fort Greene said Spike used to play sports, but no one could testify to his competence at any game. What they all agreed, however, was that when they played, Spike always somehow positioned himself in a leadership role. He'd be the guy who drew up plays in touch football or made the lineups in softball. It seemed his most memorable athletic quality was his desire for leadership.

That was one of the qualities that bonded me to him. Back at the *Amsterdam News* I'd spent a lot of time around the embryonic black independent film scene. Spike reignited my interest in film and the dynamics of race in cinema. I remember seeing Kurosawa's epic *Ran* with him up on the East Side. As a Christmas present, he gave me the film's poster, which I still have. Later we went to the first screening of Steven Spielberg's *The Color Purple* in Times Square, a film whose style and content outraged him.

When Spike was impressed, as with *Ran*, his speaking voice was deliberate and slightly hushed, and had a herky-jerky rhythm that allowed you to see his mind gathering his thoughts. When he was irritated, as with *Purple*, accusation and criticism tumbled like cereal out of a box, as his voice swelled with disdain. Spike's third gear was more mysterious. He could be deadly quiet, and then, out of the blue, pop up with a question, receive a response, and then disappear back into his cocoon.

Later, when Spike went on his publicity tour for *She's Gotta Have It*, I'd get calls from journalist friends around the country wondering if they'd offended Spike, 'cause he'd give monosyllabic answers as he gazed at them sleepy-eyed. One exasperated writer in Philly told me of Spike sitting, slumped over a table, responding to questions with all the deliberate speed of a 78 rpm recording. I'd just chuckle, knowing that the agitated intensity he displayed when angry, or the cool confidence he had on the set, was as much a part of him as this somewhat frustrating slow-motion effect. Thankfully that element of Spike's personality has receded with time, a very fortunate evolution for unsuspecting reporters.

Of course, I can't describe young Spike without his playfulness. The man's always had a wicked sense of humor that included gentle ridicule, bad puns, and inspired silliness. He'd see two girls walking together and say, "Lez be friends," and chuckle at his own bad joke. Or he'd pull out some crazy 1940s slang like "rooty patootie," or talk in that high-pitched voice that would eventually become Mr. Mars Blackmon.

Spike was also, like any young bachelor, quite interested in women. Not that he was a ladies' man. He could be funny, but in those early days he seemed more awkward than charming around women, though he did know quite a few attractive young women through NYU and the interviews he did before writing *She's Gotta Have It*. For that script he interviewed a wide range of young women about their attitudes toward sex and men, a document he shared with me. Even better, I met a lot of Spike's female friends, and was able to introduce quite a few to the joys of listening to Miles's *Sketches of Spain* while sprawled out on my living room carpet.

I first saw the landmark film on the bulky old editing machine that, along with a huge Michael Jordan poster, dominated Spike's tiny apartment. How do you sum up your first glimpse of history? Well, first you realize you haven't seen anything like it before.

Sitting on a little chair, staring into a little screen, I knew immediately that Nola Darling and her three lovers were fresh characters. These black people, collectively and as individuals, hadn't been in any films I'd ever seen. Even Spike's take on Mars, an early B-boy, was more fun than what had been presented to date in early rap/break-dancing flicks like *Breakin'*.

Moreover, Ernest Dickerson's black-and-white photography and magical framing made black people look as gorgeous as I'd ever seen them onscreen. No one had shot the streets of my Brooklyn as Dickerson had (and would again in *Do the Right Thing*.) Unlike the serious black independent shorts and documentaries I'd written about at the *Am News*, *She's Gotta Have It* was sexy and funny, and had a kind of willful artistry that made me smile. Over the next few months I harassed friends and moneyed acquaintances to come out to Brooklyn to see this magical film.

I became such a believer, I invested in the film myself, using cash I still had from the Michael Jackson bio. So I took a risk, putting a few thousand in *She's Gotta Have It*, and in Spike's vision. The odds were stacked high against him. Yes, he'd made an innovative film on no money, with the aid of a crew of gifted friends. But he had no contacts in the business, and at the time, there was absolutely no precedent for a black indie filmmaker of his generation getting a commercial release. Not since Melvin Van Peebles's 1971

Sweet Sweetback's Baadasssss Song, which he'd gotten made under the guise of a porno flick, had a film taken an African American director from nowhere to stardom. Despite my enthusiasm, there was no expectation that this little sex comedy would alter that history.

Spike knew better. At least, he acted as if he did. It's hard to articulate Spike's aura of confidence, because he rarely did. He was not one for fiery speeches or cocky pronouncements. He communicated his confidence in a number of other ways. Early on Spike gave me a film book that accompanied Wim Wenders's *Paris, Texas*, and talked about wanting to do a similar book for *She's*. The man didn't have a finished film, much less a distribution deal, and he wanted to shop a book. It seemed crazy, but at his request, we did a long interview about the film and his influences.

Spike's confidence also manifested itself in his unwillingness to compromise on creative issues. I got a major hit-making record producer to come out to Myrtle Avenue to see the film on Spike's editing machine. Then Spike and the producer came back over to my downstairs office to talk turkey. Afterward I found out that the chief topic of conversation was the jazz score by Spike's father, Bill. The record producer, like many early viewers, thought the score either limited melodically or too old-fashioned for such a contemporary feature. Spike stuck by his father and his vision. It wouldn't be the only time. Many record labels circled around *She's* once heat began to build, but Spike didn't allow a lucrative deal to ruin his movie with a hit-driven soundtrack.

The prickly shoot-yourself-with-your-mouth side of Spike would also pop up during the battle to sell the film. He had a screening of *She's* at a library on Fifty-third Street, across from the Museum of Modern Art. A white Jewish potential investor had come down to see the film and meet Spike. After the screening someone in the audience asked him about Spielberg directing *The Color Purple*.

I knew Spike hated *Purple*, but I was hoping he'd come up with some politic answer, and then move on. Instead he launched into a heated assault on Spielberg in particular, and on white directors doing black material in general. The investor was turned off by Spike's diatribe, which almost seemed his intention, as if he wished to see if the man had the proper constitution to do business with him. It was this kind of perceived race baiting that led many of his later critics to label Spike a racist, or memorably, "an Afro-fascist."

One of the challenges for any black person is negotiating his or her relationship with white power. I'd seen my mother work on the New York City Board of Education, a highly bureaucratic, totally political institution, for over twenty years and slowly move up its ranks by being a good teacher and making alliances across racial lines. My mother was a natural leader, so other teachers, white as often as black, gravitated toward her, building a support network she often tapped in to. In my adult life I'd seen that while white institutions could be unthinking, even brutal, toward black aspirations, individual whites, either through genuine friendship or political philosophy, could be crucial allies. So while I never lost sight of racism, it became a huge part of my personal development to take whites as they came, not expecting racism or prejudice from them. And even if it was there, not to overreact, but remember it and exact revenge when I could. Institutional racism was easy to scream about, but working around a prejudiced gatekeeper took more thought and was much easier if you had white allies. These truths should seem self-evident, but, coming from Brownsville and working in the eighties, it took me a while to get comfortable in the majority white situations I found myself in. Over time I took in stride the fact that many of my most determined champions and close collaborators aren't black.

So while Spike never bit his tongue on race, I never had the sense that he hated white people, judging by his long-term working relationships with *She's* editor Barry Brown; producer's rep John Pierson; producer Jon Kilik; his attorney, Martin Garbus; and many other long-standing white business partners. What made Spike mad was an American history that, close white friends aside, failed to indict white supremacy, a topic that marks his mature work as much as his floating camera shots marked his earlier.

In most successful public careers there are defining moments when that person enters the cultural consciousness. For Spike that was the 1986 Cannes Film Festival. He'd already sold *She's* to Island Films, after a successful screening at the San Francisco festival, so much of the pressure was off. He came into 19 Willoughby with six mock-ups of the poster, including the one that ended up in movie houses around the country. I threw in my two cents on which one I liked (the one he used!), and then gave Spike a couple of hundred dollars to spend in France on himself. It was probably the last time Spike Lee ever needed a loan.

By the time Spike came back from Europe, the game had changed forever. As "the black Woody Allen," he was a media sensation, and was smart enough to use that initial acclaim to build a massive career. Suddenly black nerds were chic. No longer were the only black American role models athletes, musicians, hustlers, or activists. The bookish gal, the scholarly teen, the wannabe historian, the dedicated cinephile, while praised during black history month, had rarely been icons. Spike's visibility changed that. A whole generation of filmmakers (John Singleton being the most obvious example) and smart, not streetwise, talents found in Spike a role model for success. His feisty public presence has been a necessary antidote to simplistic visions of what black success can and should be.

When *She's* opened in June 1986, Spike had an amazing party at the Puck Building on Lafayette Street in Soho. Throughout the selling of *She's* there had been a lot of parties. Often they were sneaker jams, at which folks threw down on old funk and fresh hip-hop. I had one at 19 Willoughby after a screening at the Film Forum. But this party was special, and damn near historic. In the main ballroom of the Puck Building, a long room with slick wood floors, twenty-foot-plus-high ceilings, and white columns, DJ Reggie Wells set up at the far end and threw down with Prince, Michael Jackson, classic James Brown, and new jack swing. Filmmakers, painters, rap stars, actresses, and fly folks danced hard in celebration, not just of Spike, but of themselves. It was as if *She's* was a signal that our generation had arrived, and we heeded the call by partying like *Purple Rain* extras. And there was Spike, cackling at some joke, dancing his skinny butt off and walking around with a look of deep amusement, gleefully enjoying the present and putting a nice down payment on the future.

JOKES AND SMOKE

About two years after Spike's premiere party, I was sitting in 19 Willoughby reluctantly waiting on a visitor I didn't necessarily want. A woman I'd been futilely trying to date had arranged for me to meet with a comedian pal of hers who wanted help writing a screenplay. I'd met the dude a few times before. Once was downstairs at Nell's, a hip Manhattan nightclub, where we got into an argument about music. Another time, out in LA, we found ourselves at a party both wearing *Beverly Hills Cop II* crew jackets—he'd actually been in the movie, I'd borrowed my attorney's jacket to cut the nighttime chill. Either way it was a touch awkward, and suggested the poor fashion sense we both had circa 1988.

My point is, we weren't friends, and his career was such that the idea of working with him wasn't that exciting. The comic in question had done funny things: His desire for "one rib" in *I'm Gonna Git You Sucka* was a classic bit; he'd been funny on Eddie Murphy's *Comedy Express* on HBO. But the general perception among my black entertainment peers was that Chris Rock wasn't all that funny.

Besides, I was busy. I'd recently concluded my eight years at

Billboard, and was focusing on novels, more long-form nonfiction, and a screenplay that would end up as the Halle Berry vehicle *Strictly Business*. So when this skinny, dark brown young man with a high-top fade began using his slender fingers to describe his movie, I really needed convincing. He didn't do it.

Chris had a high-concept idea: a rap *Spinal Tap*. Cool. But it quickly became apparent that he didn't have much else. Well, I had things to do, stories to write, etc. So I figured the best way to get him out of my house was to give him an assignment he wouldn't complete. I told Chris not to call me until he had the name of the movie, the name of the characters, and a few other simple but important details (like a plot, for example). Chris had put so little thought into this pitch that it was almost disrespectful, so I figured some homework would end this charade.

What I soon found out was that Mr. Rock was a counterpuncher. Challenge the man, and he'd rise to the occasion. So a day later he called me with the title, *Cell Block Four*, or *CB4*, and a series of crazy MC names inspired by N.W.A. and the emerging West Coast gangsta rap scene. To my surprise, I liked the idea, and more important, I enjoyed Chris, who was smarter and more observant of life's absurdities than I'd realized. Over the course of several months he'd stop over and we'd watch *Airplane, Meet the Ruttles, The Naked Gun*, and other parody flicks. I had no idea that those early sessions would yield not just an actual Hollywood-financed movie but a long-term friendship.

When he first came to my house, Chris was a long way from being the funniest man in America. He was still living at home with his mother in Bedford-Stuyvesant, a household superficially and fictionally known to America today via his sitcom, *Everybody Hates Chris*. The reality, when I met him, was way edgier than his hit show. His father, Julius, had been dead just a few years. He had a half brother in jail. His other brothers were either in school or struggling to get their bearings in the world. His mother, Rose, almost as tart and as sharp-witted as her comic son, was just coming to terms with life as a widow. In fact, the whole family was still very much in mourning, Chris included. The burden of being the chief money earner and de facto head of the Rock household was very present in his life.

It didn't help that his career had kind of stalled. After befriending Eddie Murphy at a New York comedy club, Chris had appeared in *Beverly Hills Cop II*, *I'm Gonna Git You Sucka*, and several *Miami Vice* episodes, along with some comic specials and in clubs nationwide. But unlike other members of Eddie's "black pack" (Arsenio Hall, Robert Townsend, Keenan and Damon Wayans), Chris's talent seemed more limited, and his prospects had dimmed.

In 1990, Chris was basically living on the road, doing unglamorous gigs in the stand-up world. He worked at comedy chains such as the Funny Bone and the Laugh Factory. He traveled to frigid midwestern towns that had comedy clubs right near the strip clubs and not far from the bowling alley. It was (is) a lonely world of Holiday Inns, commuter airlines, and McDonald's Happy Meals. I remember him calling me from Saskatoon, Saskatchewan, up in Canada. I tried to imagine Chris, with his fade haircut, red leather jacket, and jeans with holes in the knees amusing a club full of Canucks. "I'm a professional comedian," he told me that night, and that was absolutely true.

What Chris wasn't yet was an artist. His sets were incredibly erratic, swinging between the kind of raunchy pussy jokes common in the emerging hip-hop-influenced comedy clubs and really edgy material set at an abortion rally. The abortion rally bit was on the surface a sex joke premised on the ease of picking up women at an abortion rally ("Cause you know they're fucking"), but it was a dangerous one. You could hear an intake of air in comedy clubs whenever Chris said "abortion rally," and a surprised sense of relief when the punch line came, as if they were as happy for Chris for avoiding comic catastrophe as they were amused by the joke itself.

This willingness to seek out humor in uncomfortable places would become Chris's trademark, an impulse he credits Sam Kinison with inspiring. Because Chris is black, the tendency is to automatically place him in the Dick Gregory/Bill Cosby/Richard Pryor tradition, but Kinison, who Chris knew well in LA as a young comic, was a defining influence. Kinison, an ex-minister turned sacrilegious stand-up, took on God as well as man before his death in 1992, and this informed Chris's comic philosophy.

As I suggested, Chris's journey to artistic maturity was a bumpy one. From that first time he visited my apartment to *CB4*'s premiere in March 1993, he had several revelatory moments. In 1990 he auditioned for and won a spot on *Saturday Night Live*, a dream of his since the days when Eddie Murphy had used the show as a launching pad in the early eighties. The *SNL* check allowed him to move first into a small apartment, and then to two increasingly larger duplexes, within walking distance of me in Fort Greene. He used almost half of his first-year salary of ninety thousand dollars to buy a little red Corvette. As he once noted, "Between taxes and the cost of living, that meant I put myself in debt." Still, he loved that car, and would drive it, top down, through Brooklyn and Manhattan eyeing girls and blasting Prince.

The journey from my living room to getting *CB4* made actually involves two intertwined narratives: One is the nuts and bolts of our film-business education; the other was spending much of 1990 through 1993 in Los Angeles before, during, and after the riots there. That our dream was to make a film about a nasty hip-hop group residing in a low-rent suburban California town made it inevitable that our professional efforts and the anger of the city would intersect.

On one sales trip in late '89 we attended an LL Cool J show at the Universal Amphitheater. It was a young LA crowd, and as racially mixed as this city could get. As Uncle L was performing, a posse of, maybe, fifteen Crips, their blue colors no longer camouflaged under black caps, jackets, and jeans, revealed themselves. Not long afterward a scuffle ensues, and a brother in a white Le Coq Sportif sweat suit goes down. Chris and I have backstage passes, and the journalist in me drives me backstage.

Four security guards carry him through a side door and lay him on the ground. He's dark skinned, about six feet tall, with short hair, but at that moment his most distinguishing characteristic is a large red dent in his left temple. His nose and mouth, like his once white jacket, are dripping with blood.

Back inside the amphitheater the show goes on. I had found that rap crowds, from the earliest shows in Harlem right through its expansion nationwide, usually managed to ignore or emotionally distance themselves from any violence at the shows. They paid their money, and they expected their money's worth. The audience remains cool even as the Crips march down toward the front of the stage, each man grasping the shoulder of the man ahead of him. A team of fifteen security men, with thick necks and wearing white Ts, blocks them just before they reach the standing section right in front of LL. With the house lights raised and security now alert, the Crips stand on chairs and flash their gang signs toward the stage as LL rips through "Rock the Bells."

Back then it was hard for an East Coast dude like me to understand the "why" of the Bloods and the Crips. We'd had gangs in New York, on and off, for decades. But we had nothing as all-consuming and relentless as these two SoCal institutions. Considering that we were doing a parody film about a rap group from outside LA, I felt I needed to at least visit the spiritual home of West Coast rap (and its gangsta philosophy), CPT, aka Compton, California. I met a comely Creole hostess at a West Hollywood bistro who had family out there. She offered to give me a guided tour. So one Saturday afternoon in 1990 I made my first trip to the home of Snoop Dogg.

It was a forty-minute ride from West Hollywood on the Harbor Freeway, an ugly piece of eight-lane highway that likely was obsolete by the time its concrete dried. A left turn off it takes you right into two police cars parked midstreet. It's just a minor traffic accident but, after listening to N.W.A.'s first two albums, I expected the worst.

Rolling down Wilmington Boulevard, our car crosses the expanse of dirt and the train tracks featured in *Straight Outta Compton*. In a couple of blocks we hit a residential area with a car or two in the parking spaces, one of them usually a late seventies or early eighties make. Middle-aged black folk, a great many of them retirees who've lived in Compton one or two decades, live in single-story houses. There are a few mobile homes around as well. We visit my guide's aunt Dee Dee, a humorous parent of two and grandmother of seven, who's got the AC on blast as she watches *The Young and the Restless*.

Aunt Dee relocated out here in 1952 from Louisiana. There were jobs in the factories open to blacks, and she found the whites, while largely racist, were too busy enjoying the surf to be interested in lynchings. By the end of the fifties all nine of her brothers and sisters had followed her west, settling in with decent jobs that supported their growing families.

But in the seventies, the economy began to slow, and the local gangs, part of the SoCal culture since after World War II, started growing. Guns, either hunting rifles or old army revolvers, had always been around. In a city like Compton, with deep southern and western roots, gun control had never been on the agenda. However, in the last decade crack had come to the CPT, and everything had gotten meaner. Aunt Dee Dee said her neighborhood was usually quiet, in large part because there weren't any teens around. Any children we saw playing in the front yard did so "only when one of their grandparents can sit out there with them." When it was time for us to go, she asked, "Where you going? Don't just be driving around out there. It's dangerous out there."

At about 2:00 P.M. on a weekday the streets of Compton are fairly empty, though pedestrian traffic isn't exactly what Cali's about. Clusters of people, mostly men thirty years old and up, hang outside variety and liquor stores, looking much like unemployed folk in any other (African) American 'hood. We drive past Dr. Martin Luther King Hospital on Wilmington Boulevard, a place of urban legend, where it's said the army trains medics because of all the mini-AK-47 victims it treats.

Despite that sad fact, and the nihilistic images of the city spewed by Eazy-E, Ice Cube, and others about Compton, I saw no drive-bys and very few young men who fit the "gangsta, gangsta" rhetoric. But there was one tense moment. As I cruised by a beat-down house near the Watts Tower, a shirtless brother wearing a Raiders cap, a drippy Jheri curl, and black jeans stepped out of the shade of his porch and into the sun to stare at our car, which was moving slowly up his block. Truth is, I was the one who was acting suspicious, peering at him like an animal at the zoo, afraid of getting too close, yet fascinated nonetheless.

Ultimately, what I got out of the trip was how isolated Compton felt compared to the ghettos I knew in New York and elsewhere on the East Coast. Sunburned and semidesolate, Compton felt a long way from jobs, entertainment, and anything like the carefree California experience of legend. It felt segregated and forgotten, a self-contained enclave where the imaginations of MCs and the simmering anger of the streets had combined in an unexpected way to turn its limitations into a rebellious, national myth. It sure wasn't a nice place to visit, and I was damn glad I hadn't, by accident of birth, grown up there.

In the background, hovering like a darkening cloud, was the Rodney King beating and trial. You didn't need to be listening to N.W.A. or Ice-T to know that the black community of Los Angeles had fear and contempt for the LAPD and all elements of the county's law enforcement. It was a popular topic of conversation, and most locals of color, whether they lived in Inglewood or Baldwin Hills, had a bitter story or two. All during the Rodney King trial Chris and I were taking our meetings, doing rewrites, and dancing the Hollywood shuffle so hard and fast that in the spring of 1992 we felt close to getting a green light from Universal Pictures.

Which is why we were at Kennedy Airport the morning after the riot started, waiting two hours on a delayed flight to Los Angeles. To this day I'm not sure how I convinced Chris to get on that plane with me. The night before on CNN you could see stores being torched, gun shops being robbed of their deadly contents, and the beating of a white trucker by angry blacks (only later did it come to light that four black folks had rescued him). Mayor Tom Bradley, ex-cop and longtime city leader, went to the influential First A.M.E. and tried to stuff a verbal pacifier in the mouths of the discontented, but it was no match for what the Simi Valley jury had unleashed.

"There'll be an additional fifteen minutes or so on our flight today," the pilot announced as we passed over Philadelphia. "We have to go around the back way into LA—because of the ruckus going on there all flights were delayed."

As the plane came over the city about 2:30 P.M., smoke billowed up from two, three, four, seven spots out the left-side windows. On the right side I saw four others. As the plane passed over the Coliseum, a huge plume of ashy black air floated up under our right wing. We got a beautiful view of the coastline when the airship curved out over the Pacific Ocean—a route determined, I later found out, by South Central residents taking potshots at arriving planes.

As we sat on the ground for twenty-five minutes, a flight attendant told me the Beverly Center had been closed because of looting, which was significant to me for two reasons: one, that LA landmark was in an overwhelmingly white part of town, suggesting that all the robberies were being carried out by people of color; two, it meant that La Cienega Boulevard, the usual route to our hotel, was a hot spot. She also said that curfews were in effect throughout LA County.

Curbside at LAX, an Arab cabbie approached us cautiously, asking, "Where are you going?" When I told him the Mondrian Hotel on Sunset in West Hollywood, he wondered if we really wanted to stay there. It seemed that there were reports of motorists being pulled out of their cars on La Cienega south of the Beverly Center. I told him he could go any way he wanted, but I was insistent on my destination because I knew that the Mondrian provided a panoramic view of the city.

After rolling up Robertson from Culver City up to West Hollywood, and then across Sunset Boulevard, we reached the hotel, where things looked normal. From the Mondrian's restaurant terrace one can see west from the power towers of Century City across lower parts of Beverly Hills, the Wilshire District, Mid-City, Koreatown, and the cluster of skyscrapers that define downtown. Beyond those areas, some in hills, some not, were places like Inglewood, Ladera Heights, and Baldwin Hills.

For two hours I sipped cranberry juice while I watched fires rage, and then smolder. I'd count out nineteen fires, and by the time I'd run my finger across the sky, there would be two or three new ones. Hovering above the city was a thick, gray rainbow of smoke that stretched from midway in the sky down to the ground, with spirals of smoke rising like miniature tornadoes.

All around me dowdy white couples, flaxen-haired models, and hip dudes in snakeskin boots stood and pointed at them. Fire engines screamed below us. The vibe I received from the other guests was chilly. Adversity usually breeds fellowship, but no camaraderie came my way.

Friday night, a few days after the riot, and Sunset Strip is as quiet as a tomb. Chris and I hit the hotel gym, and then stand out front in our shorts, marveling at the stillness on a street we've hung out on so often. Across the street is the Comedy Store, a place whose stage Chris has walked on scores of times. He wonders how much money Pauly Shore's mother is losing.

A taxi driver sleeps in his cab. Two parking attendants chill and talk. A black hotel manager in a blue blazer walks out, looks around, and says hello. About five minutes later four county sheriffs walk up the driveway, and two blue-blazered hotel staffers greet them. The group glances our way, and one sheriff, a tall brother with a glistening dome, says, "I know him. That's Chris Rock, the actor." Five minutes later the sheriffs are gone. Riot or no riot, celebrity still meant something in LA.

On June 9 Chris and I were back at the Mondrian. Frustrated that we were still in limbo, he drove us out to the Santa Monica pier, where we played skittle and ice hockey. By the time we arrived back at the hotel there was a message from our friend and producing mentor Sean Daniel. We'd been given the green light.

So the rest of the year I worked in LA and lived at that hotel, on the often frivolous enterprise of filmmaking, backdropped by the fact that we shot much of the movie on avenues that had been on fire a few months earlier. Adams Boulevard, for example, on one end had beautiful Craftsman homes in which we shot for a day or two, but on the other end it looked as depressing as the streets of Compton.

Our fictional Locash, California, was constructed of gritty streets in LA and Culver City, and in a particularly hot, nasty little Valley town called Panorama City, a place so dry and baked, I'm convinced no cloud has ever flown over it. Though *CB4* was a foul-mouthed farce, there's more than a little truth to the desperation that underlies it. Chris and I were anxious to prove we could make movies (which, truthfully, we weren't successful at doing), and the city itself was a little disoriented, none too happy to be the center of such negative attention, but unable to truly address its own discontents.

The movie opened in March '93, and I'd trek between Brooklyn and LA heavily over the next two years, growing frustrated with my efforts to build a viable career as a screenwriter, but slowly reconnecting with my life as a journalist and author. Back in Fort Greene things were evolving. Between his film work, his *Saturday Night Live* tenure, and most profoundly, his breakthrough *Bring the Pain* special on HBO, Chris couldn't eat breakfast in peace at Mike's diner on DeKalb anymore, much less walk over the few blocks from his carriage house. Driving in the convertible made no sense, so it had to be ditched. People sought out his place to take photos outside. Much like the explosion Spike had ignited in Fort Greene a decade earlier, Chris became part of the lore of what, at the time, seemed a black cultural mecca.

Within a few years Chris's heightened celebrity would force him to move to Jersey. Spike would move to the posh Upper East Side. A lot of my peers who'd moved into the neighborhood around the same time I had had either moved to the suburbs or California. No more meetings at Cino's on Fulton Street, or house parties among people my age. Younger people and newer artists were moving in. Over on Fulton Street a spoken-word scene was hot at the new Brooklyn Moon Café, where you could see then unknown talents like Mos Def and Erykah Badu declaim poetry for an audience that finger snapped in appreciation (to keep the people living upstairs from complaining). Writers like Kevin Powell, Toure, and Colson Whitehead were building their reps living on the same streets Richard Wright had once strolled.

Things were changing in my world and mostly for the best. Using some of my movie money, I'd helped my mother move back to Newport News, Virginia, the town she'd abandoned for Brooklyn before I was born. Equally important was that she'd taken Ebony and Leigh with her, giving them a chance to grow in an area where grass, clean air, and trips to the all-American mall were commonplace. My mother and nieces would still face many challenges adjusting to a slower-paced suburban lifestyle, but this relocation, which was actually part of a historic shift of African Americans from northern big cities back to smaller southern communities, gave them all a safer, healthier life and me much-appreciated peace of mind.

I thought about moving too. Maybe get a place in Manhattan or go out to LA to capitalize on a growing movie career. My landlord wouldn't sell me the building nor would they invest in keeping the property up. Instead of moving out of Fort Greene, I moved to a similar apartment, on Fort Greene Place, around the corner from the Brooklyn Academy of Music and closer to the subway.

My last day in 19 Willoughby was incredibly sad. I knew that place was where I'd grown into an adult, blossomed as an artist, and made most of my deepest friendships. I would never be that young, ambitious, or naive again. That special twenties growth period, that time you remember fondly for the rest of your life, was over.

With all my furniture moved out, the place was as empty as the day I'd moved in. But it didn't feel empty. I could still feel it all—the books, the conversations, the sex, the laughter, the mistakes, and the dreams that had kept me up so many nights. I lit a small candle, placed it in a saucer in the center of the room, and closed the door.

LIFE SUPPORT

The morning sun poured in through the big back windows of my dining room on Fort Greene Place. I sat at my long black lacquer dining table toying with a video camera. I had it aimed at a sun-splashed chair I'd set up by a corner window. My sister was coming over, and we were going to talk, not have a fight or an argument. I wasn't hiding my valuables. I wasn't anxious that she'd ask me for money or, by signing some papers, to participate in some scam. We were going to talk just like a brother and sister should. It was the morning my career and my family history would truly come together.

I was going to interview my sister on camera, which is not how most siblings communicate, but considering our recent history, this was a huge step forward. It meant that after years of tension and silence, I was going to listen to her and try to see the world through her eyes. I hadn't done that in years. Years? Maybe never.

My buzzer rang and I went downstairs to the front door. I didn't kiss Andrea and she didn't kiss me. It had been a long time since we'd been physically affectionate with each other, but the chaste hug we shared was still progress. I closed the door and followed her upstairs.

Interviewing her was the best way I knew to find out about her, as goofy and impersonal as it sounds. Moreover, I thought that in her journey maybe there was a documentary or screenplay. Maybe I could turn her struggle into something artistic, connecting my two Brooklyns through Andrea.

My sister had been HIV-positive for a little over a decade when we sat down in 2003 for our little summit conference. During those years, my view of Andrea had shifted almost 360 degrees. So much so that I'm prepared to say that my sister's acquiring the HIV virus was one of the most *positive,* transformative experiences of her life, a statement I agree is as perverse as it is true.

Back in '92, when Andrea first told me she was HIV-positive, I was sure she'd be dead in months. She was skinny and drawn, and her usual feistiness seemed to be ebbing away. You could see her eyes and her freckles, but the rest of the face seemed to be shrinking into her skull. The previous half decade had not gone well for her. Ebony had been diagnosed with a brain tumor at age ten and had battled the fallout from that surgery all through her teen years, suffering complications that sapped her self-confidence and strength for a time. Thankfully she made a full recovery. Ma had been granted legal custody of Ebony and Leigh in a court process that was painful for all of us. Andrea had married a man named Les who had just gotten out of jail. All I could think of was how Ebony and Leigh would handle their mother's imminent death. Just minutes after she'd told me she had the HIV virus, I was already thinking of my sister in the past tense.

Andrea, however, wasn't having it. She didn't plan to die, and wouldn't give up on life. In fact, for once she embraced life with both hands, focusing all her intelligence and street smarts on survival. Les had tested positive for the HIV virus in jail. When he told her, "I knew I had it," she said. "There was no way I didn't." Andrea's next move was to the library. "First I went to the local branches in Brooklyn, and then to the main library at the Grand Army Plaza. I wanted to know everything I could about the virus. You gotta remember, back then there wasn't a lot of info out there. People were still dying."

Following her reading Andrea began seeing doctors in Brooklyn, and was disappointed to find, as she explained to my camera, "I often knew more about treatment and research into the virus than they did. No wonder black folk were dying." Shrewdly she decided, "I needed to go where the information was. I started going to the gay men's health center in the Village, getting their pamphlets and finding out what the gay men were doing. They were starting to live longer. Some of the gays called us 'Breeders,' as if women didn't belong in these places, but I didn't care. I needed to know everything they did."

Unknown to me, Andrea had volunteered for various experimental treatments. She'd decided it was better to be a guinea pig than to be a passive victim. One treatment nearly put her in the hospital, as the lining of her throat and stomach became inflamed every time she swallowed. She tossed those pills as soon as she got home, but still she wouldn't stop trying.

"I got to understand how the doses of antiviral meds were overprescribed for women," she told me. "They'd have you taking five pills of a medication based on what they'd tested on gay men. But I'm a woman. My system was different. I could feel what worked and what was too much. So I began deciding for myself how many meds to take. You gotta remember, no one knew anything about how these treatments affected women. And I knew myself better than they knew me, no matter how many tests they gave me."

Andrea's trademark willfulness wasn't just aimed at self-preservation. Despite the fact that she and her husband were both HIV-positive, Andrea was determined to have another child. My mother and I both thought she was being irresponsible and quite crazy. The truth was, she knew the odds better than we did. "At that time there was a one in four chance the baby would be born with the virus. I was willing to take that chance."

So, with a clear conscience, my sister got pregnant, and delivered Jade in October 1996, a lively little girl who was born HIV-negative. Not only did Jade give Andrea another chance at motherhood, but the pregnancy pointed her life in a new direction. "At Bellevue Hospital in Manhattan I participated in a program for women pregnant with the virus. I got to know the doctors and counselors there. I'd always stayed on top of all the treatments. I was good at talking to the other women about how to handle themselves." After Jade was born, Andrea began doing some consulting there.

Getting the virus, educating herself, and the pregnancy and birth had by 2001 transformed my sister. Drugs were out. The romance of the streets was history. She began eating well, and put on weight for the first time in her life. She began favoring gospel over R&B. She and Les—who was himself now drug-free—settled in together, building the most stable romantic relationship Andrea's ever had.

Just as pleasing to witness was how conscientious a mother Andrea was to Jade. Perhaps making up for lost time, Andrea was involved in every aspect of Jade's life, helping with homework and getting her into dancing classes, karate courses, the extracurricular works. For several years it's been a spring ritual for me to join Jade and Andrea at the Univer-Soul Circus, and a winter one for us to see Jade in *The Nutcracker*. A few years back I went to a day care center to attend Jade's graduation. To my surprise, and to that of Andrea as well, the teaching staff gave my sister an award for her contributions to the PTA. I was filled with pride, truly moved by how the teachers spoke about her.

It was a feeling that I'd have often in the weeks after our interview, as I followed her to various HIV support group meetings. After her time at Bellevue, Andrea moved on to other HIV outreach groups, including a Brooklyn-based organization where she promoted safe sex, gave out condoms, and cleared up misconceptions about how HIV is caught (and hepatitis C and D too!). To see her make her presentations and command her audiences of black and Latino women and men is to see echoes of my mother as a schoolteacher. Andrea, much like my mother, was a natural leader, whom people easily responded to. It was eerie that after all those years, and all that conflict, Ma and Andrea had ended up sharing something as important as the same blood—a gift of advocacy and instruction.

◫

I'd sold a pitch to HBO about a doing a film about contemporary race relations. Through the process of developing that idea (which in 2003 turned into the fine Jim McKay–directed *Everyday People*), I got to know the folks at HBO Films, specifically president Colin Calender and a vice president, Sam Martin, one of the few black studio executives in LA who actually gets to make movies. It took years to get *Everyday People* made, but the struggle built a bond of trust between myself and the executives there.

So when I pitched them the idea of doing an HIV film based on my sister's journey, they let me pursue it. As I'd learned in my previous film experiences, getting a movie made is like pushing a boulder up a mountain wearing roller skates. One step up can turn into three steps back in one phone call. The script, which I called *Life Support*, was spiritually and personally the right thing to do, so I laced up my skates and kept pushing that boulder.

At a certain point I, and HBO, felt we had a good script, but I didn't have a movie until Queen Latifah agreed to star in it. There were very few actresses I could see embodying Andrea's commitment, cunning, and contradictions. I needed someone who could realistically be "street," yet wasn't the over-the-top caricature Hollywood (and too many black actresses) substituted for humanity. Before Latifah had become a product spokesperson and a red carpet presence, Dana Owens had been a New York–area gal who rocked the microphone with feminist gusto.

Plus, we'd actually worked together before. Back in '93 I had written and codirected an antiviolence public service announcement that she appeared in. It was my first time directing, but she'd already been building her chops as an actress with some small film roles and her part on the sitcom *Living Single*. A reason raptors (rapper actors) are so popular is that their MC personas are usually artistic creations as well designed as a movie character. That voice that pops out of your iPod is a heightened, sometimes cartoonish version of who they truly are. It was clear to me back then that Queen Latifah/Dana Owens was well in control of that duality.

Sending the script to her agents felt like running into a brownstone's stone walls. Thankfully, during my years at *Billboard*, I'd had contact with Latifah's manager, Shakim Compare, a shrewd brother who'd grown his business alongside Latifah's career. He read the script, passed it to her, and, after some anxious weeks of waiting, set up a meeting with her at a San Fernando Valley recording studio.

My producer, Shelby Stone, and I cooled our heels in the studio's rec room, munching on pretzels, watching an NBA game, and knocking around balls on the pool table. All the while I'm in my head practicing the same speech I'd been rehearsing on the plane ride cross-country. It was passionate and intense, and proved totally unnecessary. Soon as we sat down at a patio table Dana said, "I know this woman," and that she wanted to play Ana Willis, the character based on Andrea. I was so intent on my little rap that her words, at first, flew right past me.

Not long after committing, Dana and my sister began talking on the phone, finding kinship in their shared astrology sign (Pisces), knowledge of Brooklyn streets, and sharp senses of humor. I don't know everything Andrea told Dana. The details didn't matter to me. What was crucial was that my leading lady and my sister came to an understanding of the character's motivations. Those talks gave Dana the tools she needed to build Ana Willis's world.

Andrea, along with Jade and her husband, Les, were regular visitors to the set. On the days she didn't stop by, Dana often asked about her. For Andrea, having an artist of Queen Latifah's stature play some version of her smoothed over any lingering nervousness about the project. For Dana, having Andrea around gave her a tangible touchstone to build the character upon. The genius thing was that Dana never imitated Andrea. In fact, she tapped into her own history in Brooklyn (where she'd hung out quite a bit as a teenager), and in several improv scenes, crafted dialogue that made Ana Willis different from both herself and Andrea yet still grounded in the film's rough reality. Her Screen Actors Guild, NAACP Image Award, and Golden Globe wins are all testament to Dana's magnificent performance.

My mother's voice would also be represented in the film. Anna Deavere Smith, who played my mother and is famous for her ability to imitate accents in her marvelous one-woman shows, interviewed Arizona extensively. One of the best-liked scenes in *Life Support* features Anna's character scolding her granddaughter, played by Rachel Nicks. It works powerfully, because much of that dialogue came right from my mother's mouth. There's nothing like the voice of a mother telling a child to do right to resonate with audiences.

Casting Queen Latifah was the easiest aspect of preproduction. Making Queen Latifah's schedule work was the hard part, since she had rehearsals for the movie of *Hairspray* looming, an R&B vocal tour, and sundry personal appearances already on her calendar. Because our window of opportunity with her was small, we only had a twenty-day shooting schedule, plus five weeks of prep. So there was no room for error on my part. I had to be prepared, and I had to be decisive. I also had to make sure I hired reliable department heads. Being at the center of all those decisions was new to me, and often quite challenging. Plus, I had to cast the rest of the movie at the same time, including actors to play fictional versions of my mother, my nieces, and my brother-in-law. Amazingly, it all came together, and in fact, the actual shooting was a blessed experience. For example, our able line producer, Mark Baker, got *Life Support* offices at Steiner Studios, a recently opened production facility at the Brooklyn Navy Yard not far from Fort Greene. That meant that throughout preproduction, and even on a couple of shoot days, I could walk to and from work, giving me essential moments of calm during very densely packed days.

As I've observed throughout this book, my hometown has always nurtured me, giving me an endless array of things to write about. With this film, it was my turn to give something back and capture Brooklyn's dingy majesty. The borough was changing seemingly every day as we were shooting. The gentrification that began in Park Slope and Cobble Hill had spread to my 'hood Fort Greene, as well as to Clinton Hill, Bed-Stuy, and Crown Heights. The ripple effect of monied, mostly white refugees, along with the impending construction of a score of high-rises in downtown Brooklyn, was raising rents, pushing blue-collar families out, and, in many ways, was changing the feel of large areas of the once hardscrabble borough into a place safe for lattes.

I wanted to capture some of the character I grew up with and found some unlikely touchstones. In the kitchens and dining areas of Jewish homes in Parkside, Jamaican homes in Crown Heights, and African American residences in Prospect Heights we found a remarkable sameness: big wooden breakfronts, ornate and unused display dishes, lace tablecloths, fruit-filled glass bowls, and plastic furniture covering as far as the eye could see. Some particular combination of economics and aesthetics had rendered hundreds, if not thousands, of Brooklyn homes with the same furniture and attitude. While my characters were black, they were also the working poor, just like members of the borough's other long-standing tribes, so the design of the kitchens and dining areas in *Life Support* reflected that particular unity of lifestyle.

My favorite exterior symbol of Brooklyn's ugly beauty was Atlantic Avenue, one of the borough's major thoroughfares, which runs from downtown all the way into Queens. Atlantic isn't as internationally known as Flatbush Avenue or as architecturally rich as Eastern Parkway, but I was born at a hospital on it in 1957, and for years, as I took taxis out to JFK airport, I'd seen corners and structures on Atlantic that would look great on film.

The corner of Nostrand and Atlantic in Bed-Stuy became a key location for *Life Support*. We shot outside of the Yemen Grocery Store there, as well as at a Chinese take-out spot down toward Fulton Street, and then around the corner on Atlantic at the fancifully named (and foul-smelling) Hatlantic Recording Studio. The most poetic shot in the film, beautifully framed by my director of photography, Uta Bresivitz, was a long shot of Ana Willis dragging her ever-present wheelie cart underneath the tattered tracks of the Long Island Rail Road, not far from the Atlantic Avenue hospital where I was born.

Equally pleasing was to find that Birdel's, the record shop I used to visit with my mother in the sixties, and that I later traveled to as a reporter to document the "Rapper's Delight" phenomenon in '79, was still in business; it can be seen in deep background in several Nostrand Avenue shots. Joe Long, now in his seventies, was still selling music—CDs, vinyl, even eight-tracks—which was a wonderful connection of my past to my present.

I wasn't always aware of how connected I was to some of our

locations. We were using the exterior of a technical high school a few blocks from Atlantic when Andrea walked up and reminded me that back in the seventies this institution was called Alexander Hamilton High School and we'd attended Model Cities classes there. This same building was the scene of my education in newspaper nuance almost forty summers earlier.

The most important Atlantic location was a private school located next to the elevated section of the avenue in East New York. Turned out the school was run by the ex-husband of a woman who had worked with my mother in Brooklyn schools for decades. Soon as I heard that I really wanted to shoot there. But the deal was sealed when I went up on the roof. From up there you could see the Tilden projects in the distance, a tall cluster of sixteen-story buildings where I'd lived my childhood.

In the last scene of *Life Support*, the film's emotional climax, where red balloons are released in honor of friends who've died of AIDS, the Tilden projects and all of Brownsville is visible. It was a long, hot, exhausting day shooting on that roof in late June 2006. But I did it joyfully. It felt like my life and work had, at least for those hours, come full circle, that those two threads of my life had been weaved into one thick tapestry.

The last thread was music. Maxwell's live version of "This Woman's Work" had haunted me since I first heard it on *MTV Unplugged*. Kate Bush's lyrics and Maxwell's spellbinding vocal connoted all the feelings of love and vulnerability associated with childbirth and parenthood. Even from the script stage of *Life Support* I knew this song was the perfect accompaniment for the rooftop scene.

I'd known Maxwell since before his first album was released. He'd contributed a sexy, wordless vocal to the music that supported my first serious short film, *To Be a Black Man*, a decade before. Making Maxwell's participation even sweeter was that the suave crooner was from East New York himself—another Brooklyn homeboy in thrall to music and the search for transcendence. Stuart Mathewman, the bandleader for Sade and someone I first met back in '85, not only scored *Life Support* but had worked with Maxwell on *Black Man* too. The circle was complete.

Just as the decision to write *Life Support* reclaimed my sister for me, the process of directing the film reconnected me to the streets and thoroughfares that had molded me. It was that connection that allowed me to direct the actors, edit the film, and choose the music with great clarity. *Life Support* isn't a true story. I took liberties with the characters, situations, and conflicts within my family to create a workable drama. All the lessons I'd learned in my writing career came to fruition on the film. And the fact that I wasn't a character in the story had a profound effect on me, liberating me from any self-consciousness about the material and allowing me to focus on making a film about black women, a group as consistently unrepresented and abused by filmmakers (black as well as white) as any in cinematic history.

In terms of our real life story, I wish I could report that all's well that ends well, but, after all, we're talking about family. The tensions between my mother and sister continue, and I imagine they will linger until death do them part. Ma taking custody of Ebony and Leigh was a breach of the mother-daughter bond that may never be closed. Andrea still resents it; Ma still resents having to do it. It is the manifestation of a war of wills that's not gonna end just because I made a movie about them. Movies are finite; life flows on.

Andrea can still irritate me too. But now it's just normal sibling tensions, not painful, deep-seated, or hateful. I didn't know quite where my interview with her would take me, but I do know this: Whether the script had become a movie or not, it definitely brought my sister and me back together. Now she helps decorate my apartment. I have Thanksgiving with her, Les, and Jade. I go to picnics with them. I support her. She supports me. After all these troubled years, I have a sister again.

FAMILY REUNION

It was a warm June evening out in the suburbs of Newport News, Virginia, a once sleepy southern town that in the twenty-first century had boomed with mixed residential development, big-box department stores, and high-tech businesses such as Symantec. I sat outside an Olive Garden in the middle of a sprawling strip mall, holding a small red beeper that would light up when our table was ready. My mother sat across the walkway from me on a green iron bench alongside the reason we were all here: my eighteen-year-old niece, Leigh, who was graduating from high school the next day. Her father wasn't there, but we tried to ignore that fact. Helping in that process was the man sitting next to me, Van, father of my oldest niece, Ebony, who, in the strange alchemy of father-daughter relationships, was actually closer to Leigh than he was to his own daughter. Ebony was in our little circle too, standing a bit to the side, seeming anxious for this dinner to be over. Andrea sat on another metal bench with Jade, who clung lovingly to her mother.

My father came up the walkway alongside his brother James George. They were a pair of short, compact, tough, light-skinned southern boys who had taken very divergent paths since leaving Newport News for good in the late fifties. After serving in the Korean War my father married my mother and moved to New York

City. Uncle James had stayed in the service, traveling around the world and moving patiently up the ranks.

By the eighties he was a lieutenant colonel working out of the Pentagon, and in charge of administering the Army's gigantic PX system. After leaving the service he'd started a successful computer business in the D.C.-Maryland area. All through that time he'd been married to the same woman, and had a boy and a girl. He looked fit and prosperous, despite bypass surgery a few years earlier.

Nelson Elmer, the older of the George boys by two years, never had a career, though he'd traveled widely during his peripatetic life. I could probably count the times we'd hung out during my life using my fingers and toes. In fact, as he walked toward me I couldn't remember the last time we'd had a real conversation.

Both my father and uncle wore stylish light-colored summer suits. My uncle had more hair, while my father's balding pate was shaped like my balding pate. I hugged my uncle. I shook hands with my father. Then I noticed that he was missing a lot of teeth. It was hard to believe that a man who'd been careful, almost vain, about his appearance would allow five or six of his front teeth to fall out and not be replaced. He'd been working as a security guard over the last decade. Putting it all together it meant that Nelson Elmer probably had little or no health coverage. Ergo, he had no way to fix his teeth. I tried not to focus on his mouth, which is hard when a man missing a bunch of teeth is talking to you. The nasty irony of this moment was that we were all there to celebrate the fact that Leigh planned to study dentistry in college. All weekend family members would make jokes about getting cheap dental care, or even investing in her sure-to-be-lucrative practice. Yet her grandfather walked around with a sad mouth that everyone noticed and no one had the heart to ask about. Whatever discomfort I had being around him was dissipated every time he spoke—which was often. Still, Elmer wasn't a bit self-conscious.

At a long table I found myself sitting between my mother and father, a position I couldn't recall ever being in before. The last time I was even present when my parents were in the same space was in the 812 New Jersey backyard in the eighties. Ebony was about four and Leigh was yet to be born. I took a picture of my mother and father sitting on a bench that day, which had been my only photographic evidence that the two had ever known each other. But now I'd have another. My sister had her camera. My uncle had his. In between the salads and the ribs and the large Coca-Colas, we got lots of pictures. Many smiles. Some genuine.

The next day Nelson Elmer drove my mother and me through Newport News and over to Hampton, to Leigh's graduation. Perhaps when I was two or three I'd ridden in a car with them, and maybe once or twice as an older child. What is a commonplace occurrence for most of the world was a revelation for me. In the short journey on Highway 64 through Newport News to Hampton, two small cities my mother and father had spent their childhoods in, it hit me just how lucky I was they hadn't stayed together. These two Virginia-bred, New York–seasoned folks were as incompatible as two people could be, something that had become apparent to both not long after I was born. It's fashionable (and traditional too) to argue that families, especially black families, need to stay together to raise truly healthy kids. Well, I gotta say I don't believe my life would have been as productive or fulfilling if Nelson Elmer George and Arizona Bacchus had not led separate lives.

So I sat in the backseat, a half smile on my face, as my father talked and my mother frowned. She didn't like his jokes, or his cocky attitude, and really, really hated his driving. I just sat behind them, watched this awkward scene, and chuckled to myself, acknowledging that everything had actually worked out as it was supposed to.